That's What They Are in For!

That's What They Are in For!

A Pastoral Memoir of a Privileged Profession

ROBERT E. LEVERENZ

RESOURCE *Publications* • Eugene, Oregon

THAT'S WHAT THEY ARE IN FOR!
A Pastoral Memoir of a Privileged Profession

Copyright © 2014 Robert E. Leverenz. All rights reserved. Except for brief quotations in critical publications or reviews, no part of this book may be reproduced in any manner without prior written permission from the publisher. Write: Permissions, Wipf and Stock Publishers, 199 W. 8th Ave., Suite 3, Eugene, OR 97401.

Resource Publications
An Imprint of Wipf and Stock Publishers
199 W. 8th Ave., Suite 3
Eugene, OR 97401

www.wipfandstock.com

ISBN 13: 978-1-62564-090-1

Manufactured in the U.S.A.

Thirty years of parish ministry is much like life in general;you live into it. That is how for me the story of the privileged profession came about. The journey of growing into the story has individuals who cheered me like an audience in the arena, pressing on to the prize.

It would require another volume to record the names of all who have influenced, indeed shaped my life beginning as a child in the life of the church culminating in a full life as a United Methodist pastor in local parishes. That being said there are four individuals who require mentioning having played a pivotal role in my journey.

Laura and Henry Terpening launched me on the trajectory towards a fulfilling life. Laura was the choir director at my home church Trinity Methodist Church, Kingston, New York. Music was the doorway through which I walked into my life of story telling.

The third individual is the Reverend Ivan Gossoo my home town pastor when I was in my early teens. He presented the face of the gospel in his concern for the poor. His life portrayed the prayer of St.Theresa of Avila; Christ has no body on earth but ours.

While Rev. Mr. Gossoo helped chart my course into the ranks of the clergy it was Bishop James S. Thomas who kept me on that course when doubts began to surface concerning my vocation. His understanding and response is recorded in chapter 5. His influenced on my ministry cannot be stated adequately.

For those four and all who have touched my life through the years and enabled my life to be so exiting, I give thanks to God.

A final note of thanks goes to the staff at Minuteman Printers; Tom Malone, Anna Harrison and Debbie Huckbeck who worked with the editing and preparation of the manuscript making it publishing ready.

Bob Leverenz

Contents

Foreword   *ix*

1. The Beginning   1
2. Riceville-McIntire   3
3. Grief I   7
4. Webb-Gillett Grove   15
5. Bishop James S. Thomas   25
6. Practice of Ministry   31
7. Fort Dodge   35
8. Valley United Methodist Church   43
8. St. Timothy United Methodist Church   53
9. Laurelwood United Methodist Church and Lincoln Street United Methodist Church   61
10. Faith United Methodist Church   65
11. The Architecture for Worship   69
12. Post 1962 Theological Voices   81
13. The Monastic Tradition   85
14. The World That Was My Parish   95

Contents

15	The World that Is My Parish	97
16	A Daily Focus	99
17	Discoveries	101
18	Authors and Their Influence	107
	Afterword	110

Appendixes:

A: The Episcopal Leadership   111

B: Reflections, Letters from Africa, and *The Kiterunner*   113

C: Commentaries—Public Radio KUNI, Human Sacrifice/War, and Whatever Became of Cemeteries?   121

Bibliography   129

Foreword

If you are someone thinking about becoming a parish pastor or priest, this book might assist you in your decision making.

If you are a recent graduate from a school of theology or having secured the appropriate credentials to be a pastor and approaching your first appointment or call with both excitement and a bit of anxiety, this book is for you.

If you are a seminary counselor/professor or a seasoned pastor seeking to counsel a student as to whether the parish is for her or him, this narrative might be helpful.

This literary effort is one man's testimony about the extraordinary privilege it is to be a clergyperson or priest in a local parish. The vocation of parish pastor has been for me a most exciting, humbling, fulfilling life. The story following is uniquely mine and I do not write this to bring to bear the destructive dynamic of competition with others.

For anyone who is impressed by the ministries of the church or have had disconcerting moments with pastor and parish this literary effort is for you because it helps us understand the humanity and the divinity embodied in a community of Jesus followers.

Foreword

I write this memoir for many reasons. First, I have become aware of the fact that so much written about the local church creates a picture from which one turns away. It is my hope you will believe me when I say the calling to be a local church pastor is a privileged profession permitting one to enter the very hearts of people and share their joys and their sadness. We begin with a note on the role of music in our heritage and a phrase that is identified with the United Methodist Church historically.

Our Theology in Song

Singing is as integral to our heritage as grace. We know we sing our theology and in the light of that understanding I am making note of three songs from *The Faith We Sing*, which gives us insight into the theological basis for ministry, for community, and mission and an understanding of what empowers and strengthens us to live as Jesus people in the world. These three songs with their theological dimensions I perceive as threads woven into the very fabric of this literary effort.

You are Mine #2218. "Do not be afraid I am with you. I will call you each by name. Come and follow me, I will lead you home. I love you and you are mine!"

In this selection we are told whose we are and to whom we belong. We are named. This identity is underscored by the Sacrament of Baptism.

The Servant Song #2222. "Won't you let me be your servant, let me be as Christ to you. Pray that I may have the grace, to let you be my servant too."

Once we have claimed our identity underscored by our baptism, we now discover how we are to relate to one another and to the world at large.

She Comes Sailing on the Wind #2122. "She comes sailing on the wind, her wings flashing in the sun. On a journey just begun, she flies on. And in the passing of her flight her song rings out through the night, full of laughter, full of light, she flies on."

Identity has been established. We have a clue as to how we are to live in the world, embodying the kingdom ethic, and now we find ourselves empowered by the Holy Spirit. This empowerment, the nurturing by the Holy Spirit is strengthened by the celebration of the Eucharist.

The World Is My Parish

This declaration may have lost its impact as we have sought to appropriate it for our use in the twenty-first century. The source of this declaration is said to have been found in a letter written in 1739 by John Wesley upon the occasion of his being barred from preaching in the pulpits of the Church of England. In his *Journals* he stated, "I look on all the world as my parish – thus far I mean, that, whatever part of it I am I judge it meet, right, and my bounden duty to declare unto all that are willing to hear, the glad tidings of salvation" (*Journal*, June 11, 1739). It was a statement implicitly addressing the globalization of Christianity.

Picking up on that imagery I add a nuance to it; that of a World House.

Those two images inform this literary effort to convey the challenge, the beauty, the fulfillment, the growth necessary to live this privilege profession, a local parish pastor. The World House informs the concept of a parish which incorporates the global community.

Foreword

I have discovered just how small my "world house" was and consequently "my world parish." So I invite you to come with me as I reconstruct room by room, this "world house" that has been a most privileged profession, that of a United Methodist parish pastor.

Others have sought to tell us how a world house should be built. Those efforts took and continue to take the form of a veritable cascade of writers whose books attempt to give us a panacea for a "vital congregation," a "successful congregation," a "faithful congregation," an "effective congregation," a "new emerging church congregation." Along with this cascade of books we find these "building blocks," five practices, ten guidelines, six steps, four rules, etc. One of the problems with those literary efforts is they were and are predicated on the idea that there is something "wrong," "unproductive," "ineffective," certainly "unsuccessful" with the way one is doing ministry. Now, in the twenty-first century more and more books are coming off the press written by "successful" clergy. These create a climate that does not permit the clergy to simply be her/himself, tailoring one's ministry by matching one's personality and one's gifts with the circumstances in which one is living out one's ministry. The continuous promoting of these books could keep a local pastor off balance if one does not have a sense of presence and is comfortable with one's efforts.

This appears to be all about institutional survival, no matter how it is glossed over with hyperbole. This numbers game is corroding the profession. This game reflects the values of our culture. In our consumer society, more is perceived as better. These efforts reflect the market mentality. It focuses on the "consumer." This approach tends

Foreword

to ask, "what is the niche not being met by other religious traditions? Perhaps our brand can win the day." It does not appear to be focusing on the Gospel story. With this emphasis, the clergy lives under a yoke of "guilt" because she or he is not as "effective," "successful," "vital," or "productive." If any of those terms are utilized, they need to be contextualized and linked with the particular gifts of the clergy. The clergy carries around the market pressures to "produce" according to the above criteria. The deadly nature of the market approach is spelled out in the fascinating book, *The Songs of the Mothers*, by Episcopal Bishop Joe Morris Doss. His book is a critique of the above focus. The chapter on Community (pages 239–315) addresses the market mentality in a cogent manner. Stanley Hauerwas in his book *Hannah's Child* also speaks to the market approach to the church's life (pages 258–59).

As I take my leave from this portion of the rationale for this book, I would encourage the leadership of the church to step back from the consumer model and leave the clergy alone to shape their ministry based on criteria other than the guidelines of the marketplace. Trust the Gospel story to carry the day without focusing on numbers, which of course seems to be the linchpin of institutional survival in the twenty-first century. Lest I become one of the critics on ministry I am trying to resist, I state categorically I do not expect anyone to duplicate my style of ministry with its myriad of venues, causes, or forms. Each must find her or his way in the doing of ministry. This literary effort is to be taken as an *apologia* for parish ministry, nothing more, and nothing less.

Fortunately throughout my ministry I have had the good fortune of having bishops and district superintendents who permitted me to grow into my ministry, which in retrospect proved to be compatible with my theological understanding of ministry, my personality, my particular gifts, and how these intersected with the public square. I recall no pressure to focus on numbers and to get people to become formal members of the institution. The people of the communities to whom the churches minister are to be seen as end in themselves, not a means to an end, no matter how laudable.

As the metaphor of a world house unfolds, I can say with certainty that this house is being filled with treasures, not necessarily those one stores up on earth where, as Jesus stated, "moss and rust corrupt." In these rooms treasures exist along with conversations with some of the leading theologians who have cross the landscape of my mind through the years.

In these rooms, in the conversations stands a pivotal figure, Jesus of Nazareth. He set off a counter culture revolution in which "the last shall be first and the first shall be last," and one in which we are invited to "love one's enemies." This dictum cuts across the never ending wars upon wars from which the pages of history are written in "ink blood."

Let us continue in the construction of a lifetime, the building of my "world house," and living into that world which truly became my parish.

To assist us in laying the foundation for our world house, we bow reverently in the direction of Mount Casino, Italy to receive a word from the fifth century monk, Benedict of Nursia (b. 480). He penned *The Rule of Benedict* which became the template for Western Monasticism. I shall write more about The Rule later. It

Foreword

is suffice to say much of the counsel present in The Rule transfers easily to our being the Body of Christ in the world. That counsel informs how we approach and conduct our worship experiences, how we maintained a sense of community in the face of individuals whose behavior is destructive to the life of community, the importance of prayer, the reality of humility, and so much more. Chapter 7 focusing on humility is worth the purchase of the book.

For our purposes at this point, the first words of the rule are worthy of our attention.

"Listen carefully, my child, to my instructions, and attend to them with the ear of your heart." (The Prologue, page 19)

For the purposes of this literary effort I invite you to attend to the following not only with the "ear of your heart" but with the mind of an adventurer. Along the way I have discovered what I choose to call some truths. Claim your voice. Speak your truth. Love your people well. Above all hold fast to your integrity for that is the only thing to which you have an absolute claim. These truths have informed my efforts in the "doing of ministry" in the parishes to which I was appointed. When I have been less than at my best in my efforts and perhaps hurt people along the way, I recall another premise from John Wesley. Love covers up a multitude of imperfections. So I have attempted to incarnate these truths. It is my wish that all laity, clergy and priests do the same.

The shape of my life story, the construction of my world house was created over decades of rich experiences in a host of venues. The raw materials of my life were being assembled in the early teen years of my church experience at Trinity Methodist Church, Kingston, New

Foreword

York. Trinity was a gathering of folks which began in an affluent part of the city. It became a community where poverty became the present reality. The distinct smell of poverty was evident. Because of that it had a compassionate ministry, for I was "poor folk." Little did I realize what was happening to me until years of experience gave me an historical perspective with which to understand that period of my life. The primary influence on my life during those years was a pastor named Ivan Gossoo and a choir director who discovered I could carry a tune. Mr. Gossoo currently lives in North Bennington, Vermont. He is 93 years old. He is an extraordinary human being who has made a difference in the world by having lived and helped congregations understand the reality of unconditional love rooted in the Gospel story. His ministry led me into youth camps where I experienced a spiritual awakening appropriate to teenagers.

The following narrative expands the telling, not only to seminarians but all who care deeply about the health of the parishes and the vital ministry that awaits clergy who consider this privileged profession.

Another motivating factor was an article in *The New York Times*, March 17, 2006 which examined the fact that so many seminary students were choosing not to go into parish life. It reported that half of the students graduating with a Master of Divinity are entering parish ministry. In the Religion Journal a similar statement was made. From 2000–06 the number of students earning a Master's of Divinity who intended to enter parish ministry fell about 15 per cent. Many reasons were given the validity of which is not mine to question. I can only lay out another story of

Foreword

parish ministry hoping it would motivate seminarians to revisit this most privileged vocation.

The final "push" for this literary effort came when I read an article in *The Circuit Rider*, November, December, January, 2010–2011. The editorial comment outlining the content of the publication was a most disconcerting editorial. My response to that editorial follows under the rubric of "A Letter to Seminarians." I insert it at this juncture because it gives the reader an overview of the scope of my ministry in the predominantly rural state of Iowa.

A Letter to Seminarians

They Don't Know What They Are In For!

This statement leapt from the page in the editor's column of the current issue of *The Circuit Rider*. I read it with dismay because the tone was one of condescension, cynicism, revealing a disparaging understanding of parish life and lack of respect for the laity and clergy in the parish setting. The rest of the article did nothing to mute the negative aspects of that one statement made by an older clergy. Having said that now let me tell you what they are in for dear older clergy, editor, and readers.

They are entering a most privileged vocation. They are being placed in situations of profound grief and ecstatic joy. In the land of profound grief they will sit with people "whose pain will never end" for they have experienced a longed for child being stillborn. They will sit with a couple whose one year old falls from life with sudden infant death syndrome. ***That is what they are in for.***

Foreword

They will sit with a couple whose vibrant young daughter was murdered in Chicago and years later they appear at your door because the murderer is being released from prison. ***That is what they are in for.***

They will be captured by wonder and admiration at a young teenager (college youth) losing his fight with cancer and yet makes it to worship even if he has to stand because of the pain. The elderly dying in the normal course of the aging process will visit the parsonage with frequency. Others will find strokes and heart attacks enveloping them with diminishments creating challenges which overwhelm their spirits. ***That is what they are in for.***

They will struggle with an elderly couple to understand why their son kills his wife, her boyfriend and himself. ***That is what they are in for.***

They will have the sheer joy of baptizing a baby telling the world to make way for the image of God. Weddings will bring much delight to families. Adventures with youths including camps and work camps in inner cities and the mountains of Appalachia: ***That is what they are in for.***

Most importantly they will have the privilege of being the resident theologian, story teller, representatives of the Christ. They will lead people into the country of prayer, scripture study, the monastic tradition with the focus on contemplation and silence in a most cacophonous world. ***That is what they are in for.***

They will have the privilege of shaping liturgical expressions for Christmas Eve, for Holy Week culminating with Easter and moving towards Pentecost when a reality called the Holy Spirit will find a whole new way of being

Foreword

in the world, in the community of Jesus followers. ***That is what they are in for.***

The venues of the parish pastor, of their walking about in the world will be limited by their imaginations, courage, and health. They will find themselves in hospitals, funeral homes, prisons, bars, places of business, and farms where people live out their days. Their emotional bank will be filled with joy and pain, sorrow and ecstasy, delight and frustration, elation and discouragement, missed opportunities to love their people well, making mistakes and learning how to go to their people and ask for forgiveness.

Above all they will discover that their job description consists of one mantra: "love your people well" and this will cover up a multitude of imperfections as John Wesley noted somewhere in his voluminous corpus of writings.

That is what they are in for. Tell them that!!! If you, older clergy and editors of *The Circuit Rider*, are unable to tell them that, send them to me. I will tell them.

The following narrative expands the telling, not only to seminarians, but all who care deeply about the health of the parishes and the vital ministry that awaits clergy who consider this privileged profession. The story unfolding is my journey across Iowa and how my parochial parish became one encompassing the world. The range of parishes demographically encompassed small town, rural, unincorporated village, "blue collar" community, suburbs with the profile including upwardly mobile executives, and other "white collar" workers. The last of these profiles was a university community. This variety enriched my life immensely and each provided a welcoming com-

Foreword

munity not always available to others whose employment uprooted them. The chronology of these parishes follows with each providing a milieu that challenged and nurtured me and my family. Every parish possessed a mosaic of personalities, unique cultural expressions, and diverse talents, which gave each church a distinctive face. Yet, in the midst of this mosaic, this complexity, there were threads of commonality, weavings embracing life and death, tragedy and joy, love and suffering. These are the polarities, the realities which can transform us.

As this story of the privileged profession unfolds, it is my earnest hope the reader, particularly those who might be considering entering the community of parish pastors, might be intrigued, or captured by its richness. These parishes, the gift of the people who embraced us at the door, I remember with gratitude.

> 1962–1964 Riceville/McIntire
> 1964–1968 Webb-Gillett Grove, Iowa
> 1968–1974 Fort Dodge, Iowa
> 1974–1980 West Des Moines, Iowa
> 1980–1986 Cedar Falls, Iowa
> 1998–1998 Portland, Oregon
> 2000–2007 Troutdale, Oregon

1

The Beginning

1962

The year is 1962.

The place: *King Chapel*, Cornell College, Mount Vernon, Iowa

The event: The annual meeting of the North Iowa Annual Conference.

Bishop F. Gerald Ensley is presiding.

The process leading to my ordination as a deacon was quite uncomplicated. It stands in stark contrast to the current method of "hoop jumping," which appears to be counterproductive, revealing characteristics of an interrogation, which discourages rather than nurturing and inspiring the newly called.

That's What They Are in For!

The Process

As the conference proceeded, I was invited to appear before a committee to be interviewed. Following this conversation with this committee of The Board of Ordained Ministry, I was introduced to the clergy meeting in executive session. The welcome by the assembled body was warm. Subsequently after the introduction and the appointment noted by Bishop Ensley, he said; "I bet the people of Kingston, New York don't know where Riceville-McIntire are." I agreed! Subsequently, appearing on the floor of the conference as a group, the incoming class was asked disciplinary questions, one of which was "Do you promise to visit from house to house?" The answer: "I do!" For me this question is foundational for the practice of ministry.

Not possessing a Discipline at that time, at the last minute, a gracious pastor by the name of Glenn McMichael loaned me his copy of *The Discipline of the Methodist Church*. That copy I still have in my possession.

That question was the entry point into the lives of my parishioners, the cornerstone if you will. I have no reason to believe it to be anything less than the cornerstone 50 years later. Being informed of my first assignment fresh out of seminary (Duke Divinity School), after the session ended with the "fixing of the appointments," we were on our way.

2

Riceville-McIntire

We headed for Riceville-McIntire, Iowa. Riceville was a community of approximately 1,000 folks. McIntire was a small town six miles north. This parish was located in the northeast corner of Iowa approximately 40 miles from Decorah, the home of Luther College. I note the presence of that college because in 2010, I found myself invited to the campus as a guest speaker participating in a program called "A Sense of Vocation" sponsored by the Lilly Foundation.

We approached the town from the west on Highway 9, which carried us down a hill, across a small bridge into the main street of Riceville.

Upon arrival the parish community welcomed us with gestures of hospitality which would have made St. Benedict proud. One family in particular became close friends. That friendship continues to this day.

The first parsonage was a large square house with a living room, dining room with a built in china cabinet, kitchen, and an entry way with staircase leading up to four rooms and a bath. It had hardwood floors throughout. It was a lovely house.

The Series of Firsts

The demographics of this parish extended across the age spectrum from babies and little children to elderly, retired folks. I immediately discovered there was a children's choir in both churches. This first surprise called forth my musical skills. Fortunately, being musically inclined this responsibility I welcomed comfortably. Their presence and their singing affirmed the existence of "angels" in our lives. Friendships and children's choirs in both churches confirmed the privileged status of parish pastor.

As the first Sunday drew near, the first order of worship had to be created, a homily written, the bulletin printed. This last task was done for us by the principal of the local high school. Sunday morning came. I walked across the driveway to the church, entered, and proceeded to lead the congregation through the first "date" we had with each other. I was keenly aware of my elevated level of anxiety. That awareness was confirmed by the rapid pace with which I spoke. Metaphorically speaking, it would be identified as a "bullet train" in its speed. I believe that was the shortest sermon I ever gave and one to which the congregants were attentive and gracious. It went well. A delightful time of camaraderie followed.

The memories of that parish were nurtured 40 years later when I spoke at Luther College. I was engaged in conversation with caregivers at the local hospital around the issues surrounding hospice and a "Death with Dignity" law we have in the state of Oregon. A young woman approached me and conversation revealed immediately she was a baby in the Riceville Church during my tenure, 1962–1964. A couple of days later she was able to bring her parents to Decorah and we had a lovely reunion. I was privileged to reconnect for her father was near the end of his life's journey. It was a poignant reunion.

From the presence of delightful children's choirs we travel to the other end of the age spectrum where we found many deaths in that first year. It became evident there was no retreating from this important pastoral responsibility coming my way in such large numbers. The only response to appropriate to this reality was the acceptance of it. I learned quickly the wisdom of Ecclesiastes 3:7. "There is a time to keep silent and a time to speak." The death of the elderly seen as being in the normal course of events enabled me to shape a pastoral presence which I hope was helpful. It was the unexpected tragedies that drove me into the silence where consoling words might be found. One such unexpected tragedy was the death of a youth killed in an auto accident caused by teens racing on a highway at night with their lights off, careening into the parishioner's car. The loss of a child interrupts the normal pattern of the dying process in which the parents precede the child in death. When that happens to a family it is traumatized and carries that loss throughout their lives. The grief is lifelong and intense. This awareness calls for a brief excursion into the world of grief.

3

Grief I

The power of grief can be overwhelming. C. S. Lewis, in his personal note, *A Grief Observed,* wrote of his grief when his beloved Joy died after a brief marriage of three years. He wrote, "Grief is like the sky, it covers everything." My personal experience years later confirmed that truth when my wife died in 2007.

There is no "how to" book with expressions to "pull out" and deal like a card from a deck. This is the time when God's grace can provide the appropriate response out of the silence and tears of the moment. I have tried to capture the power of grief and the severity of the loss with the following poem.

A New Club

A new club whose membership
Qualifications are ancient,
Whose rolls span the age of humankind—
Whose chapters include all forms of life.
A new / old / ancient club
Entrance to which can
Come in the speed of a heartbeat
Become quiet.

That's What They Are in For!

> A new / old / ancient club
> Entrance to which becomes
> Crowded by those who
> Traverse fields of the tragic;
> Flanders, Ypes, Verdun,
> Dresden, Hiroshima, New York,
> London, Madrid, Mumbai ...
> A new / old / ancient club
> Whose members gain entrance
> By a physician's diagnosis.
> Membership open to all,
> Experienced by all.
> A new / old / ancient club—
> The Hole in the Heart Club*
> My membership card is dated
> August 19, 2007.
> Yours?

Counsel for Parishioners

When our parishioners find themselves in a situation of grief over the loss of someone they love and don't know what to say or express concern over how to comfort one, I have learned that all we need to do is encourage people to see their role not unlike ours. There is no need to worry about saying something. I encourage them to simply "be" there. If one feels they must speak to cope with the silence, a teaching moment is before us. We can encourage them to say exactly what they are experiencing. "I don't know what to say, but I want you to know I am here." That is enough. Not everyone feels comfortable sitting in the silence. But it can be a consoling experience if we can do so with calm. The bereaved are comforted by the presence of one who cares.

Grief I

Sitting quietly in the silence seems to be a lost art in our talkative, chaotic, noisy society.

In moments such as this, lessons can be learned by being attentive to another extraordinary but neglected part of our faith tradition, namely the monastic tradition. To avail ourselves of the opportunity to walk in the corridors of the monastic silence is a privilege that is ours to receive. We shall visit that "room" later in this narrative.

In this first parish a local funeral custom came upon me unexpectedly. While visiting a family at the funeral home they proceeded to take pictures of their loved one lying in the casket. At first I found it disconcerting not having experienced this before. I learned quickly there are many local customs which might surprise me. They can enrich my life if I'm open to them and grasp the importance parishioners attach to them.

In the area of funeral practices, another first came my way. As it turned out this was the only time during my 40 years as a pastor I had the privilege of officiating at a funeral in a parishioner's home. It was a beautiful experience. It is a practice I would encourage the church to revisit. The directors of funeral homes are open to helping the families in their communities and I'm confident they would accommodate the bereaved. Since cremation has become a common practice, the presence of a casket would not be a deterrent to this venue.

A final word needs to be recorded relative to the dying. It is a privilege to be present at the bedside of a dying person. At first the experience was discomforting to this young pastor with little experience with the reality of death. But the privilege of being present and witnessing the manner in which many elderly in particular welcome this moment I consider a sacred moment. I recall a lovely elderly person in the hospital surrounded by loved ones. She faced every one of them one at a time and told them, "I love you." Then she simply rested until the end.

First Wedding—1962

The first weddings gave to me a joyful responsibility of this privileged profession. I quickly discovered another local custom of those assembled for the wedding. Throughout the service they behaved like the paparazzi at a celebrity event with their flash cameras. Before digital and video cameras, which can be utilized unobtrusively, flashbulbs were popping off in disconcerting numbers. Subsequently, at every wedding I asked the assembling guests and the official photographers to refrain from taking photos during the service. Pictures could be taken before or after the worship service. People needed to be reminded of the fact that we were in the church, with a Christian order of worship. The wedding is indeed sacred and not a stage show. People respected those instructions. It is helpful to remember our Roman Catholic friends who consider marriage a sacrament. Perhaps that perspective too needs to be revisited by the United Methodist Church. Could not the wedding ceremony be considered an outward and visible sign of an inward and spiritual grace? I believe that language is contained in the current wedding ceremony in *The United Methodist Book of Worship* and used in the liturgy of the ring exchange.

In this first parish I had the good fortune of being encouraged by the people. It is almost an axiom to state

Grief I

that the first assignment a pastor encounters will shape the pastor's ministry for years to come. The first congregation can make or break the pastor's will to serve or drive the pastor from the ranks of the clergy. They were there for the experience of the "firsts." First birth, first baptism, first confirmation, first death and funeral, first high holy days of the church year, first conflict which tests the clergy's integrity to speak and act on matters of justice in spite of the discomfort generated. It was helpful indeed to be encouraged in all those endeavors.

The First Conflict

The first conflict I encountered focused on the civil rights movement sweeping the nation, particularly in the south with the sit-ins at Greensboro, North Carolina and the boycotts in Alabama and elsewhere. My awareness of this movement became clear to me while I was at Duke. At that time a few of us participated in picketing stores in downtown Durham. Dr. Martin Luther King Jr. visited Durham during that period of time and a group of us drove across town to hear him speak to an overflow crowd in a Baptist church. The power of oratory was evident that rainy night in Durham, North Carolina.

The event in Riceville which evolved into my first conflict was the presence of a minstrel show that was going to take place in the community. I expressed my concern in the light of the larger drama taking place throughout the nation. I viewed it as another racist activity performed by whites. I considered it to be a caricature of blacks. To raise the consciousness level of my parishioners, I conducted a study of the book, *Black Like Me* by John Howard Griffin.

That's What They Are in For!

In addition to that issue the Vietnam War was beginning to heat up with all the attendant protest including the burning of draft cards. It became clear the world has a way of setting the agenda for the clergy. To that issue I gave a voice of protest as well. Not all were pleased. Little did I realize the pattern was established for my being in ministry. Not only did I see my primary role as that of a story teller and providing a pastoral presence, but I realized the clergy has to be a critic of the social order. This was a role one has to exercise in such a way that the preaching can be heard and not with such stridency that would have your people tune you out. Was I always successful in that effort? Of course not! I often heard the word prophet attached to the critic of the social order. I would caution us in the usage of that term. I believe the term is used too loosely. The use of that term calls for greatness beyond the moment and can best be interpreted by the chroniclers of history.

As I thought about the privilege accorded me in this specific vocation, the experience has guided me, metaphorically speaking, in the construction of and living within a house filled with treasures. There are rooms where conversations with some of the leading theologians took place. In these rooms one of the pivotal figures of human history lived. These conversations impressed upon me the truths of Jesus' life. Jesus of Nazareth set off a counter culture revolution as noted earlier in which the "last shall be first and the first shall be last," in which loving one's enemies cuts across the never ending paroxysm of wars upon wars writing the pages of history with blood ink.

Grief I

In these rooms celebrations of life took place, deaths were experienced, tragedies recorded. Although reference has been made to the reality of death and the power of grief, additional observations are warranted because of the heart rendering experiences that could walk into the life of a pastor. Another excursion into the world of grief follows experiences in my rural parish prompted by the tragic. Prior to that, the importance of a small occurrence needs to be noted.

In this first parish I discovered the importance of the small gesture. One day I was returning home from visiting folks and I noted a couple of young men, high school age, playing catch with a football. I made a gesture to them to toss me the ball. Fortunately I caught it with a bit of flare and threw a long pass to one of them. That brief encounter led to both of those young men attending worship from that time on. The end of the story of their young lives is not a happy one. One young man was killed in Vietnam and the other died in a car accident. The loss of these two vital young men was felt keenly by the community.

The people in this first parish taught me much about the nature of faith and a way of life fading into history. I can still see Mrs. Machin who would tell me of her comfortable conversations she had with the Lord as she rocks back and forth on her porch. An older gentleman tells me stories of his horses pulling the sled to town. Not being able to see the road buried beneath several feet of snow, he simply guided them between the fence rows. The horses portrayed in the pictures which adorned the walls of his living room were gargantuan Perchins.

4

Webb-Gillett Grove

The Construction of My World House Continues

Let us return to my second appointment. The demographics of these two small churches brought into being two extraordinary youth groups, one junior high and one senior high. To be able to work with these youths was a privilege of the first order. I recall one of activities we initiated to raise funds for UNICEF. We went to the town of Spencer, Iowa some 25 miles north. It is a community of around 10,000. We walked the main street with sandwich signs promoting shoe shines for UNICEF.

This same youth group went to the Goodwill Camp in South Sioux City, Nebraska to do repairs at the camp including shingling a roof on a cabin. Included in those two years of this work project were our visits to the city to recruit young people to attend camp.

This community of faith had within it a cadre of independent women who appreciated my efforts to make the liturgy gender inclusive. The feminist movement was alive and well years before it captured the national spotlight. This took the form of simply changing the words in

the hymns we sang and more current translations of the Bible, supplanting the King James Version. There were others who were not pleased. A lovely elderly woman with a gracious demeanor stated her displeasure pleasantly by saying, "We were here before you came Bob and we will be here long after you are gone."

A very interesting situation surfaced in one's ministry around the issue of the pastor's age. Being young, my opinions were not given the same weight an older clergy's might, as testified to by the comment one parishioner made after I expressed my point of view on a subject. "Your young, just wait until you get a little older, you will understand." I suggested to this gentleman wisdom or insight is not simply reserved for the elderly. At the other end of the age spectrum, I encountered the converse. In the midst of my ministries my energy, creativity, and ideas would bring the response, "you are so youthful in your energy and creativity." Alas, it appears creativity and energy are reserved for the young clergy and not the older clergy. Fascinating!

The second appointment brought my ministry into the tragic and the joyful with great intensity. The tragic found expression in the death of a young woman of the Webb parish being murdered in Chicago. The grief of her family was overwhelming. They were inconsolable. The emotions are raw, the feelings are intense. There one walks gently into the chambers of the broken hearts. In this situation and many others one learns how to "be." Be a quiet presence. Be a listener. Be a gentle touch, a healing hand and heart, supportive. A second and third death visited that parish with the deaths of two teenagers who died of cancer. A final sadness visited young parents whose baby

That's What They Are in For!

died of sudden infant death syndrome. I was struck by the thought that the number of these unexpected deaths were out of proportion to the size of the Webb-Gillett Grove communities of faith.

One soon learns another truth: The ways in which one experiences the loss of a loved one are inexhaustible. In this milieu, the clergy is called to incarnate the belief in a God of acceptance, love without strings attached. We are called to incarnate the loving, compassionate Christ. Should any preacher believe otherwise, that preacher needs to revisit the parable of the Prodigal Son.

Grief

Let us return once again to the reality of grief in the light of those tragic events in those two small rural churches. I begin this focus on grief with the old spiritual, "Swing Low, Sweet Chariot, Coming For To Carry Me Home." It is a spiritual of great comfort for one carried "across the Jordan" in the arms of a loving God and it speaks of the continuation of relationships, particularly the relationship symbolized by the reality of home.

> "Swing Low, Sweet Chariot,
> Coming For To Carry Me Home"

A poetic expression gives voice to my thinking about my death at this time, decades later at age 76. It speaks of experiences of death in the lives of my parishioners throughout my ministry. It speaks to the present moment while I personalize the reality of my nearing the "river's crossing."

Webb-Gillett Grove

This reality is so much closer 50 years after my ordination in 1962. This poem is a retrospect on the parish experiences noted earlier. They will become evident in the poem.

Crossing the Jordan

I wish I knew the terrain
Beyond the Jordan,
Across the Valley of the Shadow
Across the years, nearly 50,
I have escorted many to the
River's edge.
Some I accompanied:
A "stillborn,"
A baby picked up by SIDS
Teens just beginning to see the promise of a
future
Full of life, passion, intellect.
Dreamers.
At their birth the dreams are destroyed
By cancer
Murder
Auto accidents
War
Remembered only as long as loved ones
And friends choose to remember.
One exception:
A name carved on a wall of black granite
commemorating
The Vietnam War.
Along the way many lived the
Biblical dictum of 3 score and 10
And beyond
For whom death was more welcomed
Than fought against.
Some embraced the river crossing.
Others did "rage against the night."

That's What They Are in For!

> Still others could sing,
> "Swing Low, Sweet Chariot
> Coming for to carry me home."

The power of that spiritual captured in the last stanza of the poem provides great consolation to those of us who are Christ followers and go to our deaths with a dream, a hope, and assurance based on the truth articulated by our Lord in the fourteenth chapter of John's gospel narrative, in which he, too, uses the "house" motif. "In my father's house are many mansions, it were not so I would have told you. I go to prepare a place for you." Although not easily heard when one's heart is broken, perhaps in a quieter moment some consolation will be experience. One can hope so.

"Swing low, Sweet Chariot, Coming for to Carry Me Home." The privileged profession which is ours gives us this story to tell. It may not always be received, but as clergy, it is one we tell. That is what we do! As we tell the story in the presence of death, we have the richness of our tradition to comfort the mourners. The great prayer by John Henry Newman comes to us from that tradition. It underscores the truth of our Lord.

> "Lord, support us all the daylong of this troublous life;
> Until the shadows lengthen, and the evening come,
> And the busy world is hushed the fever of life is over,
> And our work is done. Then, in your great mercy,
> Grant us a safe lodging, a holy rest and peace at the last."

Because of the power of our songs, scripture, prayers such as Newman's, and other beautiful prayers in The Book of Worship, plus the telling of the resurrection motif of life, told sensitively, the very walls of this world

Webb-Gillett Grove

house, the privileged life we are building will resound not only with lamentations, but also with great hallelujahs.

As I move from the excursion into the land of grief, lamentations and hallelujahs another way of expression the hope which is ours comes from a friend, David Helms-Peyer, who for years was a pastor in the Missouri Synod Lutheran Church before he joined the United Methodist Church. At a memorial worship service of the annual meeting of the Oregon-Idaho Conference David gave the homily honoring the sisters and brothers who had died the previous year. On this occasion David was waging a battle with cancer to which he succumbed in 2005. His homily was most poignant, humorous and revealed a personal theology that gave comfort and hope to all present. From that sermon I am including a paragraph which carried us from that moment into the future in the comforting arms of a loving God from whom we cannot hide as brought to us in Psalm 139. Although his homily was wrapped in garment of Psalm 139, an important part of his testimony was in a discovery he made at seminary during a discussion of 1 Corinthians 15.

> While studying 1 Corinthians 15, one of my professors said, 'if, when we die, we discover that this business of Easter and what the church calls the resurrection of the body from the dead is just so much smoke and mirrors, so much whistling in the dark, so much trying to sweep away the high tide of death with a broom, what have we lost? At least, while stumbling along—as day follows day—we had a dream. We lived out of our dream, and we went to our graves with a smile on our faces because, we, unlike others, lived with a dream. How wonderful for us that we, at

> least, had a dream. And these saints of God had a fantastic pie-in-the-sky-by-and-by dream too. How lucky for us to be dreamers]
>
> That story, that dream, that hope from which nothing can separate us is a core component of the story we have the privilege of proclaiming and living. To affirm the hope as a dream from which nothing can separate us touches my emotions far more effectively than the creedal statements: The Nicene Creed (No. 880, The United Methodist Hymnal), "We look for the resurrection of the dead, and the life of the world to come," or in The Apostles' Creed (Nos. 881 and 882) "I believe in... the resurrection of the body and the life everlasting. Amen."
>
> With David I can now affirm, "I have a dream."

Deeper into his sermon David personalized this dream.

> Ever since 3 December 2002, Death and I have been staring each other down. Death, the last great enemy, is meandering and striding toward me, knowing full well that, from his perspective, he holds all the aces. What Death seems to be arrogantly ignorant of is that behind him and over his magnificent shoulders, I see Another. Like the father who ran to meet his prodigal son unceremoniously returning from the Far Country, rehearsed confession at the ready, so behind Death, I see Jesus, the Christ, rushing toward me arms outstretched, trying to keep from tripping over His robe, with one hand clutching his turban, laughing and singing and skipping about as if nothing were between us. And in the background I see tonight's remembered and honored sisters and brothers along with "angels

and archangels and all the company of heaven," and my mom and dad waving and cheering me on as if I were an Olympic runner entering the stadium surrounded by 10,000 times 10,000 other runners who have already finished their race and have received the glorious crown of victory. That's what I see. At least on my good days. I do this day believe and with my words, confess and, hopefully proclaim, that when we too have come to our end, we will still be where we have always been: in the arms of God.

Word and Music

The opportunities for unique experiences for a pastor seem to be always at hand. A most unusual one came to me in the form of a radio program created by the agency on communications of our Board of Education. The program was "Word and Music." This program was a service aimed at local radio stations. Local broadcasters such as I were provided with a set of records from Nashville along with a script which one could take the liberty to edit. My program aired over the local radio station in Spencer, Iowa. The narrative was interspersed with beautiful music by artists such as Leotyne Price, Mahalia Jackson, Marion Anderson, The Mormon Tabernacle Choir, Fred Warring Singers, and Robert Merrill. Over the years, 1250 scripts were created. It was a beautiful way to communicate our faith tradition. The program was well received by the listeners. There were 250 local broadcasters across the church participating in this program. It ran from 1964 to 1988. It was originally a part of the TRAFCO (Television, Radio, and Film Commission) of the National Council

That's What They Are in For!

of Churches as part of the interdenominational effort to reach out to people.

The Coaster Coffee House—Lake Okoboji, Iowa

Opportunities for ministry appear to be all about us. One such location was Lake Okoboji. A group of us Methodist clergy sought to provide a ministry to the revelers at the resort area of Lake Okoboji a few miles from Webb-Gillett Grove. We established a coffee house which involved a minimum menu; coffee, tea, and open mike, a few board games such as chess, checkers, and decks of cards were strewed about the tables. Lighted candles enhanced the milieu. We clergy would take various nights and be there for conversation and minister to needs as they occurred. I recall a very troubled young woman to whom some of us were able to relate and in concert with her psychologist from the town in which she lived we were able to provide a supportive presence for several years. In the past she had attempted suicide and was walking the edge between hope and despair. Her state of mind was fragile. In addition to being present to struggles of the youth and others, we gave musicians an opportunity to display their talents. One outstanding guitarist was a young man who played a 12 string guitar. What a privilege to be a part of something as important as a coffee house in a resort area in the summer where college youths and other young people flocked to enjoy the summer.

5

Bishop James S. Thomas

Elder Ordination in the Local Churches

During my tenure at Webb-Gillett Grove, one of the most important events of my entire ministry and in the life of those two small churches took place. It was a visit by Bishop James S. Thomas in January, 1964. The occasion was to ordain me as an elder in the Methodist Church. Also, it was a service in which Bishop Thomas baptized our first born son. A beautiful moment in that worship experience was a solo by one of the members of the Webb community. With a voice worthy of the Metropolitan Opera, she stepped forward and sang "He shall feed his flock like a shepherd" from Handel's *Messiah*. Her presentation touched our hearts.

That visit by Bishop Thomas had an additional sociological dimension to it as well; the racial component. He was the first African-American Bishop appointed to a white conference. The poignancy of the event was not lost on some of us. During my looking at the history of the Gillett Grove church, I discovered the fact that this church possessed a Bible given to them by the Ku Klux Klan. A certain amount of justice took place on that beautiful, crisp, clear day in January, 1964.

The visit of Bishop Thomas to Northwest Iowa was an event unlike any other that had taken place in those small churches. I was told that in the lifetime of those present no bishop had ever ventured to those small churches. Bishop Thomas continued that practice for several years until the number of those to be ordained elders grew too numerous to manage.

It was in this parish that I found myself feeling misplaced and having difficulty carrying out the aspects of my ministry which are most rewarding. In the midst of my struggle I was invited to the office of Bishop James S. Thomas in 1967 when he was in his first Episcopal assignment in the Iowa Conference. That conversation identified the problem. I was a man with an "urban psyche" placed in a rural milieu. Two years later, he facilitated an appointment to Fort Dodge, Iowa. That was a community of approximately 30,000. I remained in parish ministry for another 28 years. Riverside UMC was one I visited in 2012 to be a part of their 120th anniversary.

That visit was the beginning of a friendship that lasted until the death of Bishop Thomas decades later, October 12, 2010. It would be such a joy if the bishops across our institution would make it a practice to ordain elders in the local churches. One cannot underestimate the impact such a significant gesture would have on the churches. The bond between those small churches and the church at large would be enhanced immeasurably. But alas, that practice does not seem to be something that will happen in the foreseeable future. I am also aware of the truth that not all bishops display the same sensitivity towards the clergy and these small churches as that displayed by Bishop Thomas. He was a man in whose presence one became gentler as though embraced by a mantle of grace.

An additional word needs to be written about Bishop Thomas. At the creation of the Central Jurisdiction in 1939, Bishop Thomas wrote a book titled, *Methodism's Dilemma: The Central Jurisdiction*. For those who might feel far removed from that experience in the early decades of the twentieth century, an additional historical note might be helpful.

The Methodist Church / The Central Jurisdiction

An historical event of great importance took place in 1939. The Methodist Church came into being. It was the united conference at which The Methodist Episcopal Church North, The Methodist Episcopal Church South and the Protestant Methodist Church came together. The first two constituted the Methodist house divided over the slavery issue. The third player in this partnership came into being to address the question of lay leadership. As this union proceeded, something needed to be done with the African-Americans of The Methodist tradition. To accommodate the presence of African-Americans, the key issues leading to the division of the Methodist Episcopal Church North and South during the Civil War era, the Central Jurisdiction was created. As a result of that event de facto and *de jure* segregation found a home in our history to our lasting shame.

That's What They Are in For!

It is a wonder how the wheels of justice brought integration not only to the United Methodist Church in 1968, but also in the early 90s. It was a fact of life in the public square. While living in Houston I made two trips to Dallas to visit Bishop Thomas who was at that time professor emeritus at Perkins School of Theology. I will never forget the gracious reception accorded to him when we entered this lovely tea room. An elegantly attired maître de greeted us with, "Your table Bishop Thomas." I juxtaposed in my mind the hatred with which African Americans were greeted when in the 60s they had attempted to integrate restaurants.

This leads me to make additional observations about the hierarchy; the episcopacy, and the district superintendents of the United Methodist Church. In subsequent years throughout my ministry, Bishop Thomas, succeeding bishops and the district superintendents provided great encouragement and support to me in my ministry, which found itself in the midst of sufficient controversy. A pivotal conflict occurred in my appointment to Valley United Methodist Church in West Des Moines. The support I received became evident when a major conflict erupted around the issue of homosexuality. That part of the narrative we will visit later with the construction of that particular room in my "world house." It is sufficient to say I was pleased with the outcome.

It was during my tenure at Webb-Gillett Grove the Vietnam War was "heating up," the civil rights movement was in full throttle, Dr. King was assassinated, the Kennedy brothers were gunned down, and the cities were burning. The Wounded Knee episode had taken place and the Iowa Conference had aided the Native Americans in

Bishop James S. Thomas

a number of ways, including the providing of bail money for Russell Means to return from Canada for trial.

The 60s with all of those historical events drove home the truth shared in homiletics classes. The preacher needs to have a good newspaper at ones fingertips and the Bible. Connect the two. What a privilege to be thrust into the middle of such turbulence in order to help the people look at the world with a theological, gospel vision and tell the story which speaks to the world. Bishop Thomas, by his counsel, enabled me to continue to be a story teller, the resident theologian during those turbulent times. That was an era in which the world seemed to set the agenda.

6

Practice of Ministry

Story Teller

So much has changed over the fifty years of my ministry. Somewhere along the way it became clear to me what my primary role was and continues to be: that of a story teller. Although Paul spells out a number of gifts which informs the life of the Christ's followers, at core I cannot help but believe every parish pastor is a story teller and all other gifts are complementary. I want to hold fast to that truth because that is what a preacher does every Sunday: tells stories. I would encourage every parish pastor to claim that identity. Regardless of Paul's statement about being all things to all people, one thing I believe has priority: storytelling. In the order of morning worship I replaced the term sermon with, The Sharing of the Story.

The Seanishie

With the passage of the years I became more convinced of the role and the power of storytelling. What a privilege it

That's What They Are in For!

is to be a story teller. In Irish folklore and tradition of the story teller, in Gaelic, we come upon the *Seanishie (shan ah kee)*. It was an honorable calling. They enriched the lives of the Irish for centuries. One can say they could well have been the forerunners of the itinerancy. They went from village to village, rural farm home to rural farm home telling stories for their room and board. In Ireland with the telling of stories, the aura of legend and the magical wonder of myth were woven into historical moments. In the story telling you will find the uprising of the Irish against the English in 1916 Irish/Anglo War and the Civil War ending in 1922 with the division of the Emerald Isle. We now have the Republic of Ireland in the South consisting of twenty counties and the six counties in the North called Northern Ireland. This wonder and magic permeated the very air they breathed. Alas, I digress. I claim that tradition and position of Seanishie as my own.

The dynamics of local parish life has changed relative to the denomination. The population of the rural areas has diminished severely. Many moved from the rural scene to the urban population centers. The church has been placed on the margins of society due to a variety of circumstances in addition to populations movements. Except for some regional expressions, the decline is evident. It appears that the fear of institutional demise is spreading like an epidemic and is crippling the living out of this privileged profession, our ministry in the early years of the twenty-first century. As I write this narrative, there appeared an article in the *New York Times* noting the minority status of Protestants in this country and the large number of people who claim no religious affiliation

Practice of Ministry

denominationally or institutionally. With that dynamic enveloping our very being, the danger I perceive is that we will see our ministry to people as a means to institutional survival, getting them to come to church and "join" rather than as an end in themselves as noted in the introduction. It appears to me what is called for is a theology of minority status. This would be similar to the early church. We have been marginalized by our culture, but have not accepted that role.

My practice was that of calling on visitors after they had come to worship and to help them understand our ministry was always available to them even if they chose to not come and worship with us. My intention was to avoid the mantel of obligation being laid upon them. The same perspective was conveyed to members who absented themselves from worship and felt the need to "apologize" or explain why they were absent.

The idea of freedom is very important to me and in my judgment to a healthy congregation. The idea of freedom informed my relationship to our parishioners and the institution. This perspective was underscored every Sunday in our liturgy when we approached the prayer of confession. I would encourage the worshipers to take time to read the prayer of confession privately and then invite them to pray with me if they could make it their own, and to refrain from praying if they could not do so.

7

Fort Dodge

From the feed lots, the livestock of cattle, sheep, pigs, chickens, fields of corn, oats, beans, sorghum, and wheat we journey south to Fort Dodge, Iowa. Here we found ourselves in a railroad town. The culture of this community would be what is called "blue collar." Following me to this community was the reality of the Vietnam War with the protests and draft resistance. In addition to new ventures, my involvement in the protests played a prominent role. This role took place with my contact with the students at the community college not far from my parish. Fortunately, I found considerable support in my parish with this involvement.

In retrospect I perceived I was quite harsh in my preaching about the war. To this day I recall a homily given on Mother's Day. It was not my most sensitive moment. I juxtaposed the lovely aroma of beautiful flowers and the sweet smells of our world at Riverside, Fort Dodge with the aroma of burning villages and the acrid smell of burning flesh set aflame by napalm. Not everyone was pleased. I learned an important lesson from that experience. No matter how intensely one holds a position

Fort Dodge

on something as emotionally charged as the Vietnam War, with all the protests and counter protests it generated, it is not appropriate to preach a homily with such a graphic description. We do not have the right to trod over the sensitivities of the worshipers. In the parishes of that era, families had loved ones who were fighting and dying in Vietnam. This does not mean the issue cannot be addressed, but juxtaposing the plight of the mothers in Vietnam with the circumstances of the mothers in this country showed a lack of sensitivity.

My protestations about the war were rooted in extensive reading from a variety of sources, including Foreign Affairs where an analysis of our involvement in that area by Bernard Fall went back to World War II when Ho Chi Minh was our ally. Some time later the journalist died after stepping on a land mine. I was also aware of the false premise under which we entered that war with the Bay of Tonkin Resolution. Senator J. William Fulbright in his book The Arrogance of Power speaks to the bases of our involvement and his role in maneuvering the resolution through the Senate. It was a decision he came to regret (page 52). The pretense of threat was also admitted by Secretary of Defense McNamara decades later. Small consolation to the horror inflicted on the Vietnamese people and the 50,000 plus deaths of U.S. armed forces.

Night Ministry—Alcoholics Anonymous

This parish opened up to me to other avenues of ministry. One was participating in Alcoholics Anonymous (AA). In this organization of the second chance and salvation

That's What They Are in For!

(i.e. wholeness), I learned much about the illness of alcoholism. Among other things I learned there are a variety of options in dealing with alcoholism. I was impressed by the nonjudgmental flavor of AA. Ironically a second front for ministry was waiting to be acted upon. That arena of alcoholism was the locales where alcohol was sold and thus alcoholism was kept alive; the bars, taverns, lounges, clubs.

The night ministry was pushed into my consciousness by a moment of night time reflection. One evening, late at night, I was on the back deck of the parsonage overlooking the banks of the Raccoon River. Across the way lay the city of Fort Dodge. The bright lights suggested to me half the city seems to be up and about and here I was ready to retire for the evening. I and my colleagues needed to walk about in the night life of the city. A few days later I contacted some of the clergy I had met during my involvement in the Fort Dodge Council of Churches and a ministry to the bars was created. Our approach was simple. First we visited the bars, taverns, and lounges to speak with the proprietors and inform them of our intentions. We planned to simply "hang out" and engage people in conversation as they wished. We would wear our clerical collars in order to be identified. On Friday evenings six of us paired up in teams of two and visited our respective "beat."

At the end of the evening we met at a café on the square to debrief ourselves. It was interesting to note the social stratification evident in the names of the establishments. We found Joe's Place, The Brass Rail (where I sharpened my pool game), the Onyx Club and Jerry's Lounge, just to name a few that showed us the social—

Fort Dodge

economic structure of the city. Our purpose was simply to be a presence and engage folks in conversation as they chose. No agenda beyond that. We were not interested in getting people to join the church, nor to make a convert of them. We saw our role as one of simply "being a presence" to share their stories if they wished to do so and provide a pastoral response if it would be helpful. The composition of our teams was magnificent. Our group included United Methodist, Baptist, Covenant, Congregationalist (UCC), Mennonite, Lutheran, and a Roman Catholic priest. It was a rich mixture of keen minds and traditions.

Domestic Violence

The privileged trust-filled nature of this call to parish ministry took on additional dimensions when a young woman walked into my study with a baby in her arms and a little girl hanging on to her skirt. They were running from an abusive husband. The first task of a pastor on whom such trust is placed is finding her a safe place. This was managed by a phone call to an older couple in the parish who welcomed her without question. Time was bought to sort out the situation in addition to getting her safe legal counsel needed to be secured. Fortunately as a pastor the opportunity to network the city for a variety of services was a manageable task. This was done. A sensitive attorney helped her through the securing of a divorce pro bono. The end result of this woman's entrance into my study was her eventually going to college, securing a degree, seeing her children grow up in a safe environment, and eventually marrying someone who cherished her. That was not the last case of domestic violence in which

That's What They Are in For!

I have had been involved. I insert it to indicate another dimension attached to this privileged profession.

Abortion

The other issue laden with much controversy was and continues to be abortion. My first encounter with that issue came in the form of a phone call that a woman needed to speak with a clergyman. I went to the scene and upon entering the home I was met with, "I can't talk to you, you are too young." I understood and made contact with an older United Methodist Clergy in the community who followed up. Sometime later I asked my friend about the outcome of that circumstance. He stated she flew to England where an abortion was performed. The economics involved in this issue became evident. If one has financial resources, one can pretty well secure any service one wished, even an abortion. This is a fact not always noted in the heated debates around abortions.

As time went by I became a part of a group by the name of "Clergy Consultation on Problem Pregnancies." My task was to help individuals sort out the consequences of their decisions. If they pursued an abortion what would the results be? If they chose to carry the pregnancy to term what needed to be done to make it possible? What would be the worst possible scenario should they continue the pregnancy? Was a barrier one of speaking to their parents? If they wished to pursue that, I would be available to accompany them when the moment came to do such. If they were convinced in their minds to go through with the abortion, I would refer them to locations in Kansas City, Chicago or Los Angeles.

Fort Dodge

These two episodes put me in touch with the needs of women in particular. That awareness only became more fully developed as the feminist movement took hold and society at large had its consciousness level raised. Alas, the rights of women still have to be fought for these many decades later. In thinking of the heroic women around the world I am reminded of the book by Nicholas Kristoff and his wife Sheryl Wu Dunn of *The New York Times* called *Half the Sky*. The title is an ancient Chinese proverb addressing the fact that women held up half the sky.

Lighter Side

I do not wish to give the impression that this privileged profession is immersed only in the pain and the tragic of the world. There is much joy and happiness in this calling. In Fort Dodge, deep friendships were formed as was the case in the two previous appointments. Here a softball team was pulled together and we had a great time. Older couples were united in marriage. One was a divorcee and the other party a widower. A lovely experience was a congregational service for those wishing to renew their marriage vows.

A sense of community was established when the congregation found it could not afford to hire an organist or a janitor. We had volunteer musicians and the rest of us took turns cleaning the church, which consisted of the sanctuary proper, fellowship hall, gym, classrooms where the Head Start program was held. I learned how to navigate one of those industrial buffers down the stairs without doing damage to myself or the machine.

That's What They Are in For!

In this community through ecumenical contacts, a group of us created a hangout for college students. It was called "The Sit In." The building was a deserted church which we could work with at a minimum expense. The laity took the lead role in accomplishing this venture.

A final dimension to my ministry in Fort Dodge was participating in round table discussions on television. The name of the program eludes me. It was my first experience with television. This particular room in my world house was now complete and the journey to another venue and the construction of another room began. We travel from a "blue collar" profile to a "white collar" group of upward mobile executives in suburbia. Little did I realize that in this new appointment a major testing of my integrity and the mission to which we are called as Jesus' followers would take place.

8

Valley United Methodist Church

West Des Moines, Iowa

On the corner of 42nd Street and Ashworth, a new church building had just been completed and the sod was still being laid: Valley United Methodist Church. The nucleus for this church was the closing of an Evangelical Brethren Church in Des Moines. Folks from there, a cluster from West Des Moines UMC, and others in the neighborhood formed the community of Jesus' followers called Valley. The group from the EUB congregation in Des Moines was illustrative of the merger which had taken place in 1968 between The Methodist Church and the Evangelical United Brethren. The structure of this new building was octagonal in shape. It was furnished with comfortable chairs rather than pews. This provided us with flexibility in our worship setting. Since this was the only structure, the area was used for meals, theatre productions, dances as well as formal worship. Theologically speaking one can see the sacred in all these experiences.

Valley United Methodist Church

Doctor of Ministry Degree—
Christian Community

This parish provided me with an opportunity to pursue a Doctor of Ministry Degree from Saint Paul School of Theology, Kansas City, Missouri. The thesis for this project was to become a process by which the life of the Valley community was shaped for the next four years.

What constitutes Christian community? If we were able to say, these are the characteristics of a Christian community, what would they be?

This was the focus, the basic thesis for my Doctor of Ministry degree from St. Paul School of Theology, Kansas City. Because one could speak of the birth of a new community of faith in this locality, Valley's identity could be shaped. The openness and flexibility of the worship space lent itself to interaction and an awareness of each other's presence. This awareness could not be felt as keenly with the traditional arrangement of pews, providing a limited view of the other worshipers, primarily their backs. Nor could one hear one another singing in the traditional furniture arrangement. The congregation was keenly interested in pursuing this shaping of their common life as Jesus' followers.

At St. Paul School of Theology, the privilege was mine to have as mentors Dr. W. Paul Jones, Dr. Tex Sample, Dr. Marion Brown, Dr. Eugene Lowry, Dr. Bill Case, and other professors who would give occasional lectures to the doctoral students. The academic pursuit covered three years. The first year focused on profiling a Christian community. The second year took a look at our educational model focusing on the question: does our educational model enhance or diminish Christian Community? The third year looked at worship. The same question was asked: do our worship experiences enhance or diminish Christian community? Each of these foci necessitated creating a study group, presenting a prescribed reading list, and distributing a questionnaire to receive information from the community. The assessment of our education and worship models led to innovative expressions in each of those areas. One of the more important expressions in education was that of small groups meeting in the homes of parishioners, the time frame for this followed worship. The group had selective materials setting the theme for the occasion. Artistic expressions were employed such as collages, and of course refreshments were served. In addition to exploring the subject matter of the day, friendships were formed. One of the most important additions to our worship moments was the initiation of the rite of foot washing and the Seder Feast, both of which linked us with our history: the freedom march of all time, the Exodus, and the powerful symbol of servant hood.

During my tenure at Valley United Methodist Church we were able to bring distinguished guest speakers to our area in cooperation with the Des Moines District.

> Dr. William McElvaney, President of St. Paul School of Theology
>
> Dr. John Westerhoff III, Professor of Christian Education, Duke Divinity School.

These guests participated in our worship services by bringing the morning homily as well as conversations with our parishioners around the themes of the Doctor of Ministry.

Homosexuality

Valley United Methodist Church is located in a high growth area of West Des Moines. Consequently, we had a continuous stream of visitors to Valley for Sunday worship. Among the many folks who made their way to Valley UMC was a young man who became and remains a close friend since his arrival at the church in 1978. This gentleman had a keen intellect and soon moved into positions of leadership, particularly in the realm of teaching. He taught several adult classes and was a co-teacher with our high school class. One year he wrote our Lenten series and in our Christmas Desert Theatre production he played a major role in O'Henry's "The Gift of the Magi."

In the field of adult education during this period the United Methodist Church provided us with a study text titled: *"Christian Perspectives on a Variety of Lifestyles."* In that booklet there were chapters on homosexual man and homosexual woman. By this time, our friend's sexual orientation had become known. The adult class using this study text invited him to speak to their class. Other adult groups joined them on this occasion. Coincidentally, the parents of this gentleman were visiting to celebrate Mother's Day and they came to the class as well. It was an opportunity for them to help people understand what it means to be parents of a gay youth. The class experience appears to have been positive for many, although at times it became tense, almost confrontational because of comments and questions of a few individuals. Those few had a difficult time reconciling the Christian faith with approval of the homosexual orientation. Little did we realize a storm was forming on the horizon that evening.

The following Monday, an individual from that class came to see me. He demanded our friend not be permitted to continue teaching in our education program. "He was not worthy of the honor!" is the way this individual stated it. Of course that was not about to happen. In subsequent weeks the "fall out" from that class became evident. In response to that individual's demand the education committee confirmed our friend's role in teaching. Later this was endorsed by the administrative council. The end result of that endorsement was an attempt on the part of a small group to have me removed from that parish. A petition was started to gather complaints and signatures. Needless to say the attempt failed. Not for a moment did I consider leaving had the cabinet sought to respond to these detractors and appoint me elsewhere. That never became an issue for the cabinet, including the Bishop who supported my reappointment that year, 1979, and the following year 1980. It was clear to those in positions of leadership in the conference and to the vast majority of our members this was a justice issue, and the good prevailed. During the year that followed, a couple of people left Valley, but we had a considerable number of people become members of Valley United Methodist Church with full knowledge of the conflict into which they were walking. I was profoundly grateful and proud of that community of faith and its leadership. That experience was a pivotal moment in my faith journey and in the life of that congregation. With the passage of time,

Valley United Methodist Church

efforts at reconciliation were initiated. Several weeks after the Administrative Council's action, reconciliation was initiated with the worship experience focusing on the teaching of our Lord when he instructed people to leave your gift at the altar, go and be reconciled and then come and present them to God (Matthew 5:23-24). We did not receive an offering that morning. It was salutary to actually live our Lord's teaching.

With the passage of time, the importance of events seems to become prioritized. Years later, 2007, one of the primary detractors sent me a letter of condolence on the occasion of my wife's death. In that note, she thanked me for the pastoral ministry I was able to provide to her and her husband on the occasion of his having a heart attack. Once more I am reminded of the statement about love covering up a multitude of imperfections. I would add conflicts to imperfections. What a privilege to be present to another's sadness and to a gesture of reconciliation. On October 7, 2012 I had the occasion to call her and wish her happy birthday on her 85th year. She was delighted to hear from me. Among other things we discussed the conflict at Valley UMC around the issue of homosexuality. She stated: "If those circumstances were present today, it would be a non-issue." We grow in grace.

The timing of this pivotal moment in Valley's history made it possible for me to include it in my Doctor of Ministry project. It was an important expression of an inclusive Christian community, incorporating both conflict and reconciliation. The reality of conflict in this parish reminded me of the fact that many of Paul's letters were written to address conflict. Corinthians and Galatians are

That's What They Are in For!

prime examples. One need not be surprised at the presence of conflict in any congregation.

The support of the cabinet of the Iowa Conference was clearly shown in the fall of 1980. A new bishop was assigned to our conference and, subsequently, a new administrative assistant to the Bishop. The chain of events made way for a new appointment to St. Timothy UMC in Cedar Falls, Iowa. The cabinet asked me to go there. I could not have received a more overt gesture of support from the hierarchy of the Iowa Conference of the United Methodist Church.

The community of faith gathered at Valley UMC enabled me to grow in my faith and witness. It confirmed the premise that one can hold on to one's integrity in matters of justice and find affirmation. For that moment in my history I give thanks. Another room was added to my world house. It was a room in which individuals, regardless of their sexual orientation, could find a home in the United Methodist Church without sacrificing their sexual integrity. Alas, subsequent decades have revealed the truth that this acceptance is not present across the landscape of our denomination. There is much ignorance and fear surrounding this issue. It is disconcerting that our denomination does not listen to the scientific data in attempting to understand the genetic makeup of one's sexuality and refusal to study the contextual milieu of the biblical passages referencing this issue. Alas! Someday perhaps an active bishop not a retired one will take a stand definitively against the teachings of the United Methodist Church and shake it to its foundation. I know of no Martin Luther ready to stand supported by reason

Valley United Methodist Church

(including biblical scholarship) and experience against the tide of *The Discipline* and tradition.

Since that last sentence was written the Western Jurisdiction of the United Methodist Church has taken an unprecedented step towards opening up the debate on the officiating at same sex marriages and the prohibition for such found in the law book of the United Methodist Church, *The Discipline*. The Western Jurisdiction in their annual session, July 18–21, 2012, voted to extend "extravagant hospitality" to all people including "Gay, Lesbian, Bisexual, Transgender, Queer or Intersex and those whose gender expression is ambiguous."

Retired Bishop Melvin Talbert was asked to oversee a Western Jurisdiction grassroots movement that challenges bishops, clergy, laity, local churches, and ministry settings to operate as if the statement printed in the denominational law book (Paragraph 161f.) "does not exist."

Bishop Minerva Carcano, President of the Western Jurisdiction College of Bishops, said the bishops "are of one mind" during her address to the Jurisdiction.

"We believe that our beloved United Methodist Church has been less than faithful to the biblical mandate to accept all God's children including our LGBTQ brothers and sisters. We assume responsibility for preaching and teaching in every place we serve, this good news of Christ Jesus who welcomes us all," she said. Perhaps a Martin Luther has been called by God to challenge tradition.

The Northeast Jurisdiction of the United Methodist Church endorsed this position also. A group of Evangelical United Brethren in this Jurisdiction strongly opposed this and expressed disappointment.

That's What They Are in For!

The building of another room to my world house was complete. I found myself being drawn closer to the world becoming my parish in the twentieth and twenty-first centuries of the Common Era. Perhaps John Wesley might have smiled, although his autocratic ways might have placed me at odds with his leadership. That which began possibly as a cliché now was becoming a truth for me.

9

St. Timothy United Methodist Church

Cedar Falls, Iowa

The privileged nature of this profession once again was confirmed by the events at Valley United Methodist Church in West Des Moines. That confirmation became an integral part of our gospel message of inclusivity. The tent of the biblical affirmation of the worth of all human beings became larger and by implication one's sexual integrity was supported. The inclusivity of the message in the events at Valley reflected the awakening Jesus experienced in the Gospel narrative according to Mark (7:24-30). There the story is recorded of a Syrophoenician woman whose little girl was "possessed by an unclean spirit. She asked Jesus to cast out the unclean spirit. Jesus refused. He believed his message was limited to the Jews. She pushed back and turned the pejorative identity attributed to her as being a dog. "Even the dogs eat the crumbs that fall from the master's table." That exchange removed the scales from his eyes so that he now saw that God's

That's What They Are in For!

love was extended to all, Gentile as well as Jew. Perhaps someday the United Methodist Church will have the scales removed from the denominational eyes of fear and ignorance and exclusivity. The privilege is ours to provide a public forum to excise the fears and ignorance from the hearts and minds of our people and make welcome with full rights and benefits all people; lesbians, gays, bisexual, and transgender.

The granting of a public forum to proclaim such a truth was and certainly remains a privilege. The inclusive nature of our gospel outreach is needed more than ever in our day. All one has to do is reflect on the manner in which our LGBT sisters and brothers are treated in our faith community.

The building of my world house continues as we add yet another room at St. Timothy UMC in Cedar Falls, Iowa. One never knows what the Holy Spirit has in store for us as we journey to new "construction sites." Little did I realize I would find myself called to witness to the Spirit's

St. Timothy United Methodist Church

promptings in jails, prisons, the jungles of Nicaragua, through chairing the Citizens for Peace, making presentations to classes at of the University of Northern Iowa, creating commentaries for public radio (KUNI), the local newspaper with frequent commentaries, and the arena of church-state relations in the venues of the ACLU/ICLU.

1. We begin with my involvement in the prison system beginning with the country jail and extending to the minimum and medium security prisons in Iowa.

My ministry to the inmates at the county jail and prisoners in the minimum and medium prisons was the result of one layman who had been visiting the jail for some time and sought to get some help from the clergy. His name is Bill Swyers. He began attending St. Timothy and we struck up a friendship which led to my getting involved in a jail ministry, which became a regular part of my weekly visitation program. This led to the acquiring of the title chaplain which resulted in weekly prayer/bible study on Sunday afternoons. My visitation expanded from the Black Hawk County jail to the minimum security prison at Mt. Pleasant and the medium security prison at Anamosa, Iowa.

2. Chairing a peace group (Citizens for Peace)—It was a privilege to be involved with this group of activists: university professors, physicians, lawyers, women religious, and Catholic priests, housewives, students, etc. . . . This group sponsored the showing of the film *The Day After* depicting the consequences of a nuclear war. We were corresponding continually with our senators and representative in Washington on the arms race and peacemaking. We also participated in a march in Washington, DC

which included wrapping a ribbon around the Pentagon. At the local level, we participated in the annual Sturgis Falls Day parade. Sturgis Falls was the community's name prior to becoming Cedar Falls. My memories suggest there was considerable support in the community for our efforts. Of course there were detractors as well.

3. This parish provided me with the opportunity to speak to classes at the University of Northern Iowa where I sought to connect the biblical ethic to world events, notably Central America and peace issues.

4. Creating commentaries for KUNI (the local affiliate of National Public Radio) came about because one of the staff members at KUNI participated in our peace group. During this four year period, I learned to write succinctly. The radio broadcaster who assisted me helped me to realize that when you are on the air for three minutes it is imperative you capture the listener with the first couple of sentences. Those I presented ranged from the death penalty to the right wing in politics, suicide, movie reviews, and book burnings by "Christians," the Holocaust, politics and politicians, guns, and so much more. As I reviewed these it was striking to realize that so little has changed since the 80s on these key issues. I have included some of these in Addendum C to confirm the important idea that some "battles" have to be fought over and over again. Some issues appear to be built into the human DNA.

5. My tenure at St. Timothy UMC found me making a trip to Nicaragua on a Witness for Peace mission. This program was created when it was discovered that the presence of Americans in the northern region of Nicaragua armed

conflict ceased along the border with Honduras. The lull in the fighting accompanying our presence enabled the farmers to harvest their coffee crop. Consequently, groups were rotated into the area every couple of weeks. This episode took place during the conflict between the Contra forces and the Sandinista.

Our involvement in Nicaragua was typical of our involvement in Central America in that time frame including the coup we engineered under the Eisenhower administration to overthrow the duly elected President of Guatemala. Subsequently, Guatemala suffered years of civil war with the casualties in the thousands. In 2013 General Rios Montt was brought to trial on charges of genocide and crimes against humanity. Our involvement in El Salvador also left our hands bloodstained. El Salvador witnessed the murder of the Jesuits and their housekeepers at the Jesuit school in San Salvador. As recently as 2010 the perpetrators of those murders were brought to justice. Five women religious were also killed during this period. To my knowledge those who killed those women have not been brought to justice. That record of involvement in Central America and the arms race during the Reagan years provided the backdrop for the existence of Citizens for Peace and Witness for Peace.

6. In Cedar Falls, I found myself caught up in church/state issues when challenging the practice of having a Christian clergy offer an invocation and benediction at a public high school graduation. The fact that my son was a senior in high school put me in a position to participate in the graduation service at the high school with the responsibility of bringing the invocation and the benedic-

tion to the occasion. I declined the opportunity and wrote a column for the local newspaper stating my refusal to participate and I gave the reasons for my decision. Not everyone in my parish was pleased.

7. It wasn't long before the Iowa Civil Liberties Union contacted me and asked me to be a witness in a similar case being tried in southern Iowa. I was willing to do so. As I observed the proceedings in that case, it was clear that the ICLU attorney, who was accustomed to this type of litigation, was too much for the attorney representing the school system. On May 9th, 1985 Chief Judge Harold Vietor of the U. S. District Court of Southern Iowa issued an injunction against the Central Community School District of Decatur County. The judgment prohibited the inclusion of a religious invocation and benediction in the high school commencement exercises which took place on Sunday, May 12, 1985. Whether participating in that type of proceeding can be considered a privilege or not, it is imperative the clergy not be fearful of being involved in church-state issues. Stating the case for church-state separation is more important than ever in our multi-faith country.

To be able to look at the world theologically and make connections between the biblical story with its prophetic witness and our Lord's focus on the marginalized, plus the invitation to be peace makers, is indeed a privilege.

All of this and more would have been impossible without the support of friends, loving critics, and trying to keep the center in place by practicing the disciplines of piety and frequent visits to the Trappist Monastery, New

St. Timothy United Methodist Church

Melleray Abbey at Peosta, Iowa. During the tenure at St. Timothy I had the privilege of creating exciting confirmation classes with the help of laity and camp experiences for several years running with two creative, clergy colleagues, Doug Peters and Dave Crow. It was an exercise in experiential education, activity oriented. For example; when we celebrated the resurrection story from John's narrative, we had a fish fry on the beach and read the narrative of the "last breakfast." What a privilege to seek to influence several hundred young people with counter culture values rooted in the biblical story and the monastic tradition. Besides, it was fun. What other profession has that opportunity?

10

Laurelwood United Methodist Church and Lincoln Street United Methodist Church

Portland, Oregon

The appointment to Laurelwood and Lincoln Street United Methodist Churches came during my employment at Aging and Disability Services of Multnomah County. There was a sadness enveloping the Laurelwood Church. The building was very large and difficult to maintain by the handful of folks who attended there. The lower level was rented out to a school. Following my tenure the parish continued under the leadership of two pastors subsequently. Eventually the church was closed and the building now houses a school. It is poignant to see church buildings outlast the viability of the community. Perhaps the very existence of the buildings can play the role, possibly of the "stones crying out" in Jesus' reference when

Laurelwood and Lincoln Street United Methodist Churches

he entered Jerusalem that Palm Sunday long ago (Luke 19:37–40). These buildings make a silent witness to the Divine, even as human voices go silent.

Churches built many decades ago have succumbed to the cultural shift relegating formal religion to the margins of society, at least relative to the historic traditions, such as the United Methodist denomination. It is at times such as this the leadership must help the remnant celebrate what has been and lead them into a new future with other congregations or new configurations for ministry. Not an easy task. Fortunately, the gospel story continues to be told in the lives of the communicants and they find new ways of worshiping even if that worshiping community reflects the statement of our Lord: "When two or three are gathered together in my name, there I am in the midst of them." Lincoln Street UMC continues to be a lively community of the faithful to this day. For that we can be thankful.

11

Faith United Methodist Church

Troutdale, Oregon 2001–2007

The years 1990–2000 found me employed in the field of social work subsequent to my securing a Masters of Social Work Degree from the University of Iowa. In the spring of 2000 I returned to my first vocational love: being a pastor in a local parish, in this case the beloved community of Faith United Methodist Church, Troutdale, Oregon.

After leaving my position with Multnomah County prior to the gathering of the Oregon-Idaho Conference, I was asked by the District Superintendent if I would consent to be appointed to Faith United Methodist Church, Troutdale. I was delighted to be asked and accepted the appointment gladly. For me, Sunday morning worship was probably the most fulfilling experience of the entire week. The leading of worship and the sharing of the story brought me great delight. That appointment turned out to be one of the most fulfilling appointments of my ministerial career. I was able to initiate ministries I had not considered previously for reasons which elude me.

That's What They Are in For!

Celebrating the Eucharist

My first Sunday at Faith revealed to me we had a congregation that loved to sing.

Consequently, from that Sunday on we celebrated the Eucharist twice a month with a sung liturgy. It was inspiring. Our pianists/organists were very competent and were in tune with the spoken and sung word. The people of the parish were open to the liturgical pattern which I brought to them. As noted earlier, the pattern was from chapter 6 of Isaiah, the vision of Isaiah. The congregants came to realize we were worshiping within the vision. It was beautiful.

The Blessing of the Animals

When October rolled around we were given the opportunity to acknowledge the Feast Day of St. Francis of Assisi. We participated in the blessing of the animals. The day brought cats and dogs, hamsters and birds. Some brought pictures of their animal friends to be blessed in absentia. A liturgy was created and the result was an appreciation of those fur and feather friends who bring so much pleasure to our lives. The service linked us with the vulnerable among us and helped us appreciate the comfort they bring to so many. That feast day was celebrated each of the six years of my tenure at Faith UMC. What a joy!

The Personal

On a personal note, the Faith community proved itself to be an accurate representative of a loving community when my wife was diagnosed with lung cancer. They proved to be compassionate and concerned without overwhelming us. They were present to me following her death in 2007. For that support I give thanks.

Islam

The tragedy of September 11, 2001 called upon the clergy to help their congregants to understand Islam. Prior to 9/11, that area of study was not a present reality for many of us. Fortunately, I not only had the opportunity to lead such a study, but I had the privilege of participating in a two year study at Trinity Cathedral in Portland. It was called "The Abrahamic Initiative." At each meeting, an issue was placed before us and representatives of the three faiths (Jewish, Christian, and Moslem) discussed the issue among themselves. After their exchanges, the public was invited to ask questions and make observations. Along

That's What They Are in For!

with these discussions a scholar was brought to Trinity from Harvard. His name is Ali Asani. He is an Islamic scholar whose presentations were extremely helpful in giving us a broad picture of the varied expressions of Islam. As with any faith tradition, the expressions ranged from the ultraconservative, rigid fundamentalists to the most moderate. An important part of the learning experience came about with a visit to a mosque and a temple.

12

The Architecture for Worship

The Liturgy

Faith UMC was constructed by the members. They made comfortable chairs for the sanctuary as well. The absence of pews lined out like benches in a courtroom was a welcomed sight. In addition to the aesthetics of these chairs, the flexibility granted was beneficial as well, for we were able to worship as a community gathered around tables decorated with lovely cloths, candles, and flowers. How I wish such beauty could be found in all sanctuaries. If the architectural design does not readily create the reality of beauty, it could still be present with lovely vestments, flowers, and candles. It may be a matter of personal taste, but in my experience in too many sanctuaries screens descend, movie clips are shown, and clergy in blue jeans and sneakers serve the Eucharist, creating an environment challenging my sense of the aesthetics and creation of a sense of reverence. Undoubtedly, while I question its absence of a sense of dignity and beauty, it could well speak to other worshipers and for that I need to give thanks. Having said that, I would contend something is missing when beauty is not present and obvious to the eye and touching the heart. I believe the human spirit requires beauty and it is the responsibility of the pastor to see to it that beauty embraces the worshipers. It is imperative that within the limits of our situations we are called to create an environment of beauty.

While building this world house and giving authenticity to John Wesley's dictum, The World Is My Parish, I discovered certain features which need to be expanded upon. These include the role of the Eucharist in our tradition, importance of an order of worship that reflects movement and cultivates a sense of the sacred, consistency in the weekly order of worship, the conducting of worship with a sense of dignity, and the need for beauty. While the monastic tradition helped restore the importance of silence and simplicity in our lives, the reality of silence needs to be recovered in the worshiping community as well.

The thinness of our liturgical expressions with the absence of the biblical texts in too many United Methodist Churches is unfortunate. Actually, it is shameful. The responsibility for changing this sad state of affairs begins with the Bishops. They can initiate a program to help people understand the importance of a liturgy that brings a sense of reverence, awe, wonder, and beauty, as well as being informative, including frequent celebration of the Eucharist. The people will follow if the clergy lead.

The Architecture for Worship

The Face of Worship

As preparation for this literary effort, I read some of my earliest homilies and orders of worship. Immediately I became keenly aware of the language used 50 years ago. My prayers were filled with the language of King James Version with thees and thous. The importance of gender designation was beginning to surface. My language was rooted in the patriarchal culture. I remember, with the shaking of the head, a conference held in Iowa focusing on the feminization of the clergy. Amazing how insensitive we were and still are in some areas. My consciousness raising improved as the years went by.

At the beginning of my ministry, I fell back on the use of the lectionary as it appeared in *The Book of Worship*. This happened because I had to face my first Sunday with the question, "What will I preach about next Sunday and the next and the next?" It was my good fortune to have been exposed to the lectionary while at Duke Divinity School. The biblical record has a way of being relevant (blessed word) to us in the twenty-first century. It is imperative that the full range of scripture be shared with our people each Lord's Day. That is the only way some folks will hear the entire biblical story over a three year cycle.

In this regard Abraham Heschel takes us to task in his book of important essays: *Moral Audacity and Spiritual Courage.* In two essays, he speaks to the absence of the Hebrew Scripture in Protestant worship. The absence deprives the worshipers of the roots of our tradition. The story is incomplete. Because of this, the listener is not exposed to the full narrative of divine involvement in the history of a particular people and how through the centuries their understanding of the Divine, YHWH, moved upon their lives through the events and pivotal figures such as the prophets. Also, it is imperative the scripture be read well so the story can be heard clearly.

The Eucharist

In the churches I visited when I no longer was in a leadership role, I experienced sadness by what appears to be the loss of much dignity, beauty, and sacredness. It seems the Eucharist has fallen upon difficult days. In many of our churches, it is celebrated quarterly. In others, the Eucharist is celebrated once a month. This occasional celebration of the Eucharist had its beginning during the days of the Circuit Rider on the frontier.

It was John Wesley's position that only ordained clergy could celebrate the Eucharist. With the scarcity of such it would be celebrated when the Circuit Riders appeared on the scene. Months would pass without the presence of a Methodist Circuit Rider. Of course this would lead to the occasional celebration. This did not change, even with the passage of time and the increase number of ordained clergy. A study was initiated at the 2004 General Conference which focused on the Eucharist. A recommendation resulting from that study was that the Eucharist be celebrated more frequently, if not weekly. Many of the laity appeared to be longing to experience the Eucharist more frequently. It is the core sacrament of our tradition, the importance of which was clearly underscored by John Wesley. Alas, it has lost its significance for many of us who are the practitioners of our tradition. It

The Architecture for Worship

can be recovered, but it would require a concerted effort on the part of the bishops to initiate it, promote it, and assist in the implementation of the Eucharist by reminding the local clergy of its importance. It would require intentionality on the part of the clergy. The effort would be worth it once the initial resistance and a lack of understanding of its significance are overcome. The Eucharist could be seen as a uniting sacrament. We would be sharing "One Bread, One Body" as our hymn tells us. We could be united in this way and on all else differ. This awareness could bring about a healing of the painful divisions within our denomination. I know many clergy would encourage it but they may need support from their colleagues to push back the fear of worship services extending beyond the 60 minute time frame. I'm afraid the hesitancy of the clergy displays a lack of confidence in the congregants to accept that which would nurture their spirits. I find it beyond my comprehension to be controlled by the clock.

The Tyranny of Time

I plea with all clergy: Do not be concerned about the length of the service. I am saddened by the fact the clergy too often are intimidated by the clock, tyrannized by time. Worship experiences are cut short, the Eucharist avoided because "it takes too much time." The importance of scripture readings each Sunday including the Psalm, the Hebrew Scripture, the Epistle and the Gospel is sacrificed. Perhaps the clergy do not have a sense of the importance of worship. Do they perceive it as something to just get through? To cut out a passage of scripture because "we

That's What They Are in For!

are running late" is unacceptable. In my judgment, the congregation would have their faith nurtured by the full complement of texts.

The lectionary would carry the day if the clergy would take the time to follow the three year cycle. The congregants are deprived of hearing the story in its fullness. I believe the worshipers would cherish exposure to the full narrative of the Bible structured in the lectionary. For encouragement to utilize the lectionary and the weekly celebration of the Eucharist, we simply need to look towards the sacramental communions like the Roman Catholics, the Lutherans, and the Episcopalians. Could it be too many clergy do not want to expend the energy to bring the Eucharist back to front and center in our worshiping community?

I encountered a counterpoint to the tyranny of time while on a retreat on Cape Cod in Barnstable. I happened upon a restaurant which was once a church. The narthex had a few tables and chairs around the perimeter. There was a counter separating the narthex from the nave where the kitchen was located. The dialogue which took place between the customers and the staff suggested it was a delightful neighborhood coffee shop. What caught my attention was a sign on the wall which could well be placed at the entrance to the nave in our churches as a defiant statement against the tyranny of time. The sign read, "If you are in a hurry you have come to the wrong place." This bit of advice would free the congregants to permit the Holy Spirit to do her thing.

Perhaps my assessment of what constitutes a significant worship experience is out of touch with the casualness and folksy attempts to make worship "relevant"

The Architecture for Worship

in our time. I tend to think not, for I look at the staying power of the Mass and the dignified manner in which it is conducted; beauty, pageantry, reverence, and worshipful, reverential manner in which the communicants approach the sacrament of the Eucharist.

We need to pay attention to the Presbyterian theologian John Killinger when he tells us people learn more about God from their attendance at worship than in the reading of books of theology.

In the city of Brugge, Belgium you will find Saint Walbugha Church. At the entrance in the narthex you will find the following inscription on a plaque. It is positioned in such a way you cannot avoid it. It speaks to this matter of having a sense of reverence in this sacred space.

Enter this door

As if the floor
within were gold
And every wall
Of jewels all
Of wealth untold
As if a choir
In robes of fire
Were singing here,
Nor shout nor rush
But hush:
For God is here!

I realize this is but one person's opinion. However, I would like to believe an approach to worship with that inscription engraved upon our hearts would assist us in experiencing a sense of the holy. But alas! I am most fortunate to have discovered in my class on worship at Duke a pattern for worship which has movement appropriate

That's What They Are in For!

for the approach to the Divine Mystery, as well as psychological, therapeutic movement.

One Worship Model—Isaiah 6:1–8

My theological education at Duke Divinity School provided me with the tools for ministry. It was my task to put those tools to good use. My class focusing on worship gave me the format I have used throughout my entire ministry.

It is found in the chapter 6 of Isaiah. The movement of Isaiah has its echo in the Mass of the Roman Catholic Church as well.

Isaiah's vision

In the year that King Uzziah died
I saw the Lord sitting upon a throne,
High and lifted up;
And his train filled the temple.
Above him stood the seraphim;
Each had six wings;
With two he covered his face,
And with two he covered his fee,
And with two he flew.
And one called to another and said;
"Holy, holy, holy is the Lord of hosts;
The whole earth is full of his glory."
And the foundations of the thresholds
Shook at the sound of the voice
Of him who called and
The house was filled with smoke.
And I said:
"Woe is me! For I am lost;
For I am a man of unclean lips,
And I dwell in the midst of a people

The Architecture for Worship

> Of unclean lips;
> For my eyes have seen the King,
> The Lord of hosts!"
> Then flew one of the seraphim
> To me, having in his hand a burning coal
> Which he had taken with tongs from
> The altar.
> And he touched my mouth and said
> "Behold
> This has touched your lips,
> Your guilt is taken away,
> And your sins are forgiven."
> And I heard the voice of the Lord saying,
> "Whom shall I send, and who will go for us?"

Along with this commitment, instructions are given to Isaiah to carry the message from the Lord. The people of my parishes have been led to realize each Lord's Day we were worshiping inside the vision of Isaiah. From worship, we go out into the world where during the week we incarnate the Christ. This understanding was captured beautifully by St. Teresa of Avila.

BEING THE BODY OF CHRIST IN THE WORLD

> "Christ has no body now but yours.
> No hands, no feet on earth, but yours.
> Yours eyes are the eyes through which
> Christ looks Compassion on the world.
> Yours are the feet
> With which Christ walks to do good.
> Yours are the hands
> With which Christ blesses the world."
> St. Teresa of Avila
> b. 3/28/1515 - d. 10/04/1582

That's What They Are in For!

That prayer was embodied in the last congregation I was privileged to serve. The Faith community at Troutdale had an amazing ministry for such a small congregation. They participated in a program that housed homeless families for a week as part of a rotation of five or six congregations. Families would come on a Sunday afternoon and cots would be set up in the sanctuary and the classrooms. Up to fifteen persons were welcomed at a time. A breakfast and evening meal would be provided as well as sleeping accommodations. After one week they would be taken to another church for similar service. During the day the families would go to a center run by a social service agency, which also provided social workers to assist them in getting housing and perhaps a job as well. The goal was to assist them in getting back into the mainstream of society.

In addition to that important program, three to five individuals would go into downtown Portland once a month to serve meals at a mission. It was a privilege to be a part of a congregation that helped the pastor to be the body of Christ in the world.

Privilege of Writing

One of the gifts given to us in this privileged profession is the freedom to write with an eye to touching the hearts of our people with the power of words. Of course this finds expression in the prayers we write, the sermons and most certainly the weekly or monthly essays which are sent to our parishioners.

The Architecture for Worship

During my decades in this privileged profession I paid close attention to the prayers I wrote on behalf of the worshiper. The creating of prayers and printing them in the order of service enabled the worshipers to participate at appropriate junctures with the liturgical refrain, "Hear our prayer O Lord." Having them printed also let the congregants know there was a beginning and an end and they contained some coherence with the rest of the service.

My monthly Reflections (Addendum B), written while at Faith UMC, gave me an opportunity to address important subjects at length. These were one page commentaries on events of the time, or a sentence from a novel that touches all of us, or reflections from abroad while traveling in England and Ireland. One Reflection was inspired by a sentence from the novel *The Kite Runner*, "There is a way to be good again!" That sentence is one which all of us can take to heart in the midst of our lives where we have been hurt by another or have inflicted another with hurt. These Reflections brought news from a refugee camps in Uganda from a Jesuit priest, and an exposition on the issue of homosexuality, bringing to bear upon it the quadrilateral of our tradition. I was able to write about a 98 year old woman of the parish whose life focused on the education of children and the treatment of women. A poem of hers focusing on the teaching and sharing of wisdom with one's words and one's life catches her flavor.

Words

Thoughts—feelings—
Written—said—read,
Shared in a quick glance,

That's What They Are in For!

> Lie fallow in rich
> Soil of a growing child.
> Even or good they will
> Expand
> Becoming a part of the
> Learner—
> Mirroring the soul
> Of the teacher.
> Percie Miles
> June 23, 1987

A second opportunity for writing about the world and communicating it to the public at large was afforded me by KUNI, the public radio station broadcast from the campus of the University of Northern Iowa. I have attached the list of these 75 commentaries (Addendum C). I have included the printing of a couple in full.

What a privilege to be in a profession that enables me to read, write, and create worship experiences for our sisters and brothers in Christ.

13

Post 1962 Theological Voices

Clergy are expected to read, to keep informed about what is going on in the field of theology, and biblical studies as well as to keep abreast of what is going on in the world so that we can assist the congregation to view the world with the "eyes" of theological understanding. The preacher has the honor of sharing this understanding with the congregation. In this regard it was energizing to "hear" some of the new voices of theology.

The world that was my parish knew nothing, formally identified as liberation theology, feminist theology, and theology of the black experience, theology of sexual minorities such as our gay brothers and sisters, and Celtic Spirituality which gives a beautiful theological framework to current environmental concerns (creation). These and so many variations on the theme impacted my life. One in particular calls for a reading.

In the book, *Freeing Theology: The Essentials of Theology in Feminist Perspective*, Susan A. Ross has an essay "God's Embodiment and Women." In it she references a poem by Frances Croake Frank which poignantly encourages us to look at the Eucharist from the experience of women.

> Did the woman say,
> When she held him for the first time in the
> dark of a stable,
> After the pain and the bleeding and the crying,
> "This is my body, this is my blood"?
> Did the woman say,
> When she held him for the last time in the dark
> rain on a hilltop,
> After the pain and the bleeding and the dying,
> "This is my body, this is my blood"?
> Well that she said it to him then,
> For dry old men,
> Brocaded robes belying barrenness,
> Ordain that she not say it for him now.

The world that was my parish knew nothing of the women's experience embracing the Eucharist. As I was thinking about her powerful statement the thought came to me. What if at every birth the mother would say "this is my body, this is my blood." It would be so significant and beautiful to wrap the birth in sacramental cloths. Would this perspective bring a new dimension of depths to the sacrament of Baptism?

Her theological, sacramental perspective found parallels in the feminist movement n the culture at large. A song which underscores the breath of the movement is titled "Sometimes I Wish My Eyes Hadn't Been Opened" by Carol Etzler. The four verses of this song call all of us, men as well as women to open our eyes to the injustice experienced by women at the hands of our patriarchal culture. And once we do that we can no longer look away.

Black Theologians included James Cone, Howard Thurman, Martin Luther King, Jr., Professors at Iliff: Vincent Harding, Edward P. Antonio.

Liberation theologians were prominent during the 80s bringing the wrath of the Vatican down on their heads: Gustavo Guitterrez, Leonardo Buff, Segundo, as well as Anglo, Robert McAfee Brown who wrote Theology in a New Key. How ironic it is that with the election of Pope Francis the focus of liberation theology is experiencing a rebirth with his call to identify with the poor clearly depicted in his recent visit to Brazil, 2013. Francis of Assisi has found powerful voice in Pope Francis

14

The Monastic Tradition

The monastic tradition is a neglected aspect of our heritage. It is one to which I believe it would be nurturing to return. This chapter begins with an important understanding of the monastic's daily activities as well as a listing of the hours. The schedule is one I have experienced in the monasteries in Iowa, Oregon, England, and in Rostrevor, Northern Ireland.

Schedule of Daily Activity

"Life in the monastery is an education of the heart that transforms the lives of community members into the image and likeness of God. Prayer—personal, reflective prayer as well as community prayer—lies at the heart of monastic life and is essential to the rhythm of the monastic day. A typical day for the monks at New Melleray and the list of monasteries below begin long before dawn.

3:15 a.m.	Rise
3:30 a.m.	Office of Vigils
4:15 a.m.	Breakfast, prayer and reading
6:30 a.m.	Lauds

That's What They Are in For!

7:00 a.m.	Eucharist
9:15 a.m.	Terce, followed by morning work
11:45 a.m.	Sext
Noon	Dinner
1:45 p.m.	None, followed by afternoon work
4:30 p.m.	Prayer and reading
5:30 p.m.	Vespers
6:00 p.m.	Supper
7:30 p.m.	Compline, followed by rest

New Melleray Abbey, Peosta, Iowa
Our Lady of Guadalupe, Lafayette, Oregon
Rostrevor Abbey, Northern Ireland
St. Michaels, Farnsborough, England
The Rule of Benedict—He was born 480 CE.
W. Paul Jones—Father Paul, Hermitage,
Assumption Abbey, Ava, Missouri

In the early years of my ministry I was invited to join a group of clergy for a three day retreat at the Trappist Monastery, New Melleray Abbey, Peosta, Iowa. That invitation ushered me into a part of the Christian tradition about which I knew very little. It was the beginning of a lifelong relationship which continues to this day.

From the vantage point of years, I lament the absence of a course focusing on the monastic tradition while at Duke. I am of the opinion that this focus benefits greatly the parish pastor for it would provide a tradition and indeed a place for centering. All who expose themselves to the monastic tradition might recover an appreciation of silence. One would experience the beauty of chanting the Psalms and other refrains for the respective hours. A perspective on what is essential in our privileged profession might be discovered. I found it to be so.

The Monastic Tradition

Permit me to introduce some of the monastics who impressed me by their piety. I remember Father Willie, whose presence displayed a form of humility and piety, which was attractive. He had a soft manner of speaking. His voice disarmed one's resistance to the piety he embodied. His attentiveness was captivating. The dialogue was helpful in one's search for an authentic spiritual discipline. On one occasion a gentleman from one of my parishes was assessing his values, his life. He accompanied me to New Melleray. An opportunity was provided to visit with Father Willie. He was touched by the gentle piety of Father Willie who helped him explore his priorities. It was a transforming moment for him.

With fondness I remember other monastic seekers after God: Brother Jim, Brother Gus, Father Pius, and most of all Father Xavier whom I last visited October 31, 2012. At New Melleray I learned and experienced the importance of silence in one's spiritual development and since I am an individual who "thinks out loud" to gain understanding by talking about a subject, being silent was a challenge. My visitation to the monastery overflowed into my parish life in the act of inviting groups to accompany me to experience the gift of silence, thus becoming aware of the rich tradition which was theirs also. On one of the visits, a group of us were in dialogue with Father Tom who spoke a profound truth which we in The United Methodist Church might think about as we face diminishing numbers and influence. We seem to have succumbed to the values of the culture with numbers and bigness as the focus. When asked about the future of New Melleray in the light of the diminishing numbers of monks he stated the following:

That's What They Are in For!

"The Holy Spirit has called us into existence and when the Holy Spirit feels we have completed our work we will accept that and move on."

That is one of the truths I have shared with my parishioners over the years. That belief is such a liberating truth. It becomes a matter of faith to trust the Spirit's leading and embrace the temporary nature of our existence and indeed all our endeavors.

Another practice which informs my prayer life daily is the refrain the monks chanted at Compline the monastic hour which ushers the monastics to sleep:

> "Into your hands O Lord,
> I commend my Spirit."

In life or in death and sleep can be perceived as a moment of death, the monks seek to place themselves into the hands of God. This refrain became one I say nightly as one of my spiritual practices. Each night I pray, "Into your hands O Lord, I commend my Spirit." Following that I commend into God's keeping loved ones and those with special needs.

The monastic lifestyle reminded me of how few things are necessary to live a life of meaning. Simplicity was practiced by the monastics long before the depletion of our planet's resources has compelled us to consider a simpler lifestyle.

Illustrative of this is the directives concerning clothing. In *The Rule of Benedict*, chapter 55, we find the quantity, quality, and type of garment the monks are permitted. He made arrangements for every contingency, including the weather.

The Monastic Tradition

The counter culture values of the monastic tradition became a permanent point of reference for my living out of my ministry. The monastics embrace cooperation rather than competition, community rather than individualism, and interdependency rather than independence. The first time I found these contrasting values spelled out was in a paper by Dr. W. Paul Jones when he became attracted to the monastic life after attending the Trappist Monastery at Snow Mass, Colorado (The Christian Century, May 31, 1972). Much has happened in Dr. Jones' life since that visit to Snow Mass. He wrote about that experience in *The Land Beyond the River*. Dr. Jones' life has been transformed by his exposure to the monastic tradition. For a period of time he sought to divide his time between his teaching responsibilities at the seminary and the monastery. Finally, he made the decision to leave his position at St. Paul School of Theology, Kansas City, Missouri and become a Roman Catholic priest, and then a Trappist Monk. He is now residing in a hermitage linked to Assumption Abbey in Ava, Missouri. His powerful narrative of that journey is contained in the book, *Teaching the Dead Bird How to Sing*. To experience his presentations in class as a part of my Doctor of Ministry program was an informative, intense event. His teachings were an authentic representation of how he lived life in the economically deprived section of Kansas City.

While at New Melleray I entered into the silence surrounding me, the wind whose presence was recognized in the swaying of the pine trees and the wheat fields. At these moments my pen hurried across the page, giving visual expression to the observed. I recalled Jesus' statement that the Spirit blows where it will. We don't know

That's What They Are in For!

where it comes from or where it goes but its presence is undeniable. So it is with the wind, a reality I sought to capture in the poem that follow.

Walking in the Game Refuge

I stood on a rise in the midst of a great expanse
And the feeling gave rise to the thought of
The potential expansiveness which can belong to a
Generous and gracious heart.
As the wind blew I remembered
Jesus' words about the Spirit blowing
Consciously letting the wind caress me.
Aware of its power . . .
Its apparent invisibility and yet
Grasses bent in the wind
The pines provided strings across which
The wind would play as a bow . . .
The need for something to be "in the way of the wind"
In order to give the wind identity:
That is suggestive . . .
The Spirit will be without identity until it touches
A life and that life becomes a witness to the Spirit's
presence. . .much like the waving prairie grasses
And stately pines become witnesses to
The wind's presence . . .
Lord, we wait the blowing of the wind
The wind of your spirit . . .
Its source and destination remain a mystery,
But its presence can be known in women and
men of faith. Amen.
New Melleray Abbey, Peosta, Iowa
October 28, 1980

The sign posted on a tree telling visitors the monastery lands were off limits to hunting found the poetic muse within giving verse to the sign.

The Monastic Tradition

GAME REFUGE/NO HUNTING

Lord, as I wandered in this "Game Refuge"
It occurred to me that this perspective
Could be helpful in our viewing one another.
Sign on the earth: "Human Refuge/No Hunting"
Certainly this could apply to the
Community of friends gathered in your name,
The Church.
Sign on the door: "Human Refuge/No Hunting"
No hunting to find the place to hurt another,
No hunting to say the destructive word,
To act in a way that manipulates another,
Controls another.
A chance to care,
A chance to love,
A chance to be a presence against,
And to speak a word in opposition to
Violence, personal and corporate.
Those are the features which belong
To the Community of Friends.
Human refuge!
A place where life is preserved.
No Hunting!
New Melleray Abbey, Peosta, Iowa
October 28, 1980

This is the world that is becoming my parish in the twenty-first century. It is a world full of meaning, calling me to a global consciousness, to work towards the creation of a new humanity, a World House, big enough to house all religious traditions, not just my tribal expression of the Jesus people, The United Methodist.

For that I am most grateful!!

This exposure to the monastic tradition enabled me to venture abroad to the monastery in Rostrevor, Northern Ireland. The monks were sent to Northern

That's What They Are in For!

Ireland in 1989. It became too dangerous for them to remain there. They returned to France. In 1998 they were sent back to Northern Ireland to work on reconciliation between Protestants and Roman Catholics. A modest monastery was built at Rostrevor. I was received with hospitality that touched the heart. To give you a flavor of that experience and how it has the capacity to nurture one's spirit I want to insert in the narrative my experience at Rostrevor. It is a *Reflection* I sent to my parishioners from Ireland.

Come with me to the picturesque Kilbroney valley near Rostrevor, Ireland. There you will find a new Benedictine monastery. It is the first to be built in Ireland since 1183. This Holy Cross Benedictine Monastery was completed in 2003. Why such a place in the twenty-first century and in that location?

"Our particular mission is to contribute to the reconciliation between Catholics and Protestants in a land marked by reciprocal violence, stained by the blood of Christian brothers and sisters," stated Father Mark-Ephrem, the Superior of the five member community. The monks will contribute to the climate of reconciliation by their presence, prayer, and the promotion of dialogue between and among the various religious traditions in Northern Ireland. Alas, while at Rostrevor I was hoping to visit the local Methodist pastor. It was relayed to me that on an occasion of dedicating a new facility at the Presbyterian Church the Methodist clergy chose not to come. He stated: "I don't pray with Catholics." How pathetic.

The experience of Benedictine hospitality at mealtime was heartwarming. At dinner the tables are ar-

The Monastic Tradition

ranged in a horseshoe pattern. The Abbot, Father Mark, and another monk sit at the closed end of the horseshoe. Behind them is a large window presenting us with an unobstructed view of the valley in which the monastery is located. The valley floor arrayed with fields, rock walls, sheep grazing, wind break arrangements of willow trees scattered about the grounds give way to the forested hills beyond. The hills are set against a beautiful blue sky.

As we sit in complete silence (a requirement throughout the monastery extended even to guests), beautiful music is playing in the background. The only conversation one is having is that carried out in one's mind. The meal is served by the monks in this sacred environment. The *entre* is a salmon loaf over which a light cream is ladled. Noodles are served to compliment the salmon. Along with this, because this is a feast day (the feast day of the Birth of the Virgin Mary), wine is offered. For desert we had a palate-pleasing bread pudding with a meringue on top, to which ice cream was added. The quiet, the music, the view, these enhance the experience of eating.

The "Monastic Hours" (worship opportunities during the day beginning at 6:45 am) end with Compline. It is now 9:30 pm. The day has ended. Walk with me out of doors. Let us wander the grounds. It is a beautiful moonlit night. The stars are scattered like ornaments across the black/blue sky. The wisps of clouds are illuminated by the full moon. This is a night made for reflection, for being immersed in its beauty. Ah yes, I would be remiss if I did not say it is a night made for romance. The sounds playing upon our ears are simply the sounds of the fields and woods, including the breeze working its way through the

That's What They Are in For!

trees. A few distant lights flickering from the farmhouses scatter the darkness, if only in small segments. To be in this valley at night immersed in moonlight and to be able to recover the gift of silence portrayed by the monks in this beautiful setting provided me with a moment in which the heart is nurtured. The gift of silence I fear is one from which we run too often. Such is the nature of a place dedicated to communion with God. Here one embraces the possibility of having a greater appreciation of the beauty of creation, of being a little kinder, a little more generous in acceptance of others, a little more forgiving knowing one's own need for such, a little gentler and more tender of heart, of speech and hopefully, of action. This is a place where the streams do sing and the trees do dance and "clap their hands."

15

The World That Was My Parish

The world that was my parish did not know of HIV/AIDS and the churches response to that pandemic that is still going strong in some areas of the world.

The world that was my parish did not know the pain and oppressive milieu, culture of the sexual minorities; gay/lesbian/bi/transgender worlds of my friends.

The world that was my parish knew very little about the monastic tradition, the rich heritage of prayer, and the counter cultural values of the monastic tradition: cooperation, dependency, community; contrary to the values of the culture (individualism, competition, and independency).

If we touched on that rich heritage in my Church History course, it was just that, a light touch, which made no indentation on my knowledge base.

In this arena the world that was my parish did not know or study "The Rule of Benedict," the template for the monastic tradition of the Western World. I highly recommend reading and living with "*The Rule of Benedict; Insight for the Ages*" by Joan Chittister, a Benedictine Abbess from Erie, Pennsylvania. It is one we read and

That's What They Are in For!

reflected upon in my parish. And groups from my parish made trips to Our Lady of Guadalupe in Fayette, Oregon. And many from my parishes in Iowa have journeyed to New Melleray Abbey, near Peosta, Iowa (ten miles or so west of Dubuque).

All this and more have given meaning to my life. As I live in the matrix of these ecumenical expressions the small one room house in the World House kept getting bigger and bigger.

The world that was my parish knew nothing of Thomas Merton, Henri Nouwen, the mystics such as Teresa of Avila, St. John of the Cross, Teresa of Lisieux, Julian of Norwich, Catherine of Sienna, to name a few. Vatican II had not taken place.

The world that was my parish knew very little about the world's religions, although I did have a cursory understanding of Buddhism, Hinduism, and Islam. Also, I had a deeper understanding of Judaism, our heritage. Karen Armstrong and Huston Smith had not walked across my horizon, the landscape of my mind. Now I believe I can claim Wesley's dictum as my own and write about the world that really is my parish.

16

The World that Is My Parish

The world that is my parish has all of the above within it that was absent when I began my ministry with Wesley's dictum echoing in my mind: "The world is my parish."

The world that is my parish today has within it an extensive study of the Abrahamic Initiative; a two year study of Judaism, Christianity, and Islam at Trinity Episcopal Cathedral, Portland, Oregon. In this program there were scholars from the three traditions speaking to us on common themes each week. They would interact with one another and then open the discussion for audience participation.

Listening to Ali Asani, a Muslim and Islamic Scholar from Harvard has given me an understanding of the many rooms in the house of Islam, from the open, receptive, flexible most accepting Muslims to the Taliban. I drew parallels, where possible to those who claim absolute status to their belief system and basically writing off all others. In our faith tradition we experience those who cling to truths as though theirs is the only truth and teach an exclusionary faith.

That's What They Are in For!

These are the folks; bless them, who do not have the capacity to spread the truth of the Divine Mystery across the landscape of all religious traditions. Indeed, they have shut out any new understanding.

As my ecumenical or world house has gotten larger, so has my heart space and mind space, enriching my life with meaning.

The world that is my parish lived out in the milieu of HIV/AIDS in Houston for six plus years has helped me see the inclusive theology embracing expressions of love within the community of the sexual minorities, even giving me the privilege of honoring them with marriage ceremonies.

The world that is my parish includes the election of Gene Robinson to the Episcopacy of the Episcopal Church, USA.

The world that is my parish includes having a Muslim couple come and bring the morning homily to my parishioners, visiting a mosque and Jewish temples, and Buddhist friends; all these who dwell in the world house have enriched the meaning of my life.

The world that is my parish has the Archbishop of Canterbury speaking at Lourdes about the importance of Mary. His being their added to my appreciation of the Mother of Our Lord and the role she has played in the history of our faith through the centuries.

17

A Daily Focus

Bringing some of these discoveries home to the daily I begin many of my days listening to a beautiful soprano voice singing "The Deer's Song." It is a Celtic prayer said to be one of those on the breastplate of St. Patrick. My daily practices are The Deer's Cry focuses on the strength of heaven with all the elements addressed: sun, moon, fire, lighting, wind, sea, earth and rock. It then goes on to speak of the strength which comes from God. It closes with the encircling of the pilgrim with the Christ: within, before, behind, beneath, above, on both sides, when lying down and sitting. It is a comfortable image portrayed, going through the world enveloped in the Christ. My daily practices were also informed by selections from Thomas Merton's *Book of Hours* and *The Rule of Benedict*, Joan Chittister, O. S. B. ed.

18

Discoveries

1. Early in my journey, I discovered what I considered my primary responsibility to be that of a story teller. Years later I discovered an insight given by the Irish author Frank Delaney. In his book The Last Storyteller he writes, "If we are to live good lives we have to tell ourselves our own story." Adding a nuance to that insight, the writing of my story at this time has enabled me to determine if I have lived a good life. I believe I have, but perhaps the final imprimatur belongs to others. Perhaps others might be encouraged to tell themselves their own story in the moment and not in retrospect at the nadir of one's life.

I did not see myself as a professional counselor, although the pastor is one of the first professionals a troubled person would seek out and over the years I developed expertise in that area, particularly in responding to concerns not requiring a professional counselor such as a psychologist or psychiatrist. In several parishes, I was fortunate to have important professional relationships available.

Neither did I see myself as an administrator, although one does considerable administrating. Nor did

That's What They Are in For!

I perceive myself to be a business person or fund raiser. There were individuals in my pastorates who were competent in that field.

2. From the vantage point of years in parish ministry, a cautionary note needs to be raised. Do not let the church become your "lover," i.e. a third party in your marriage. It is a privileged profession, but it can also be a seductive one which calls one away from boundaries in responsibilities. Be attentive to your partner. If you are an extrovert as I am, it is addictive to be engaged with folks at every turn for it is in engagement we are energized and nurtured. The family can be the core of concentric circles spreading globally from the center.

3. As a pastor I wanted to be a most graceful person. Being graceful does not mean being silent in the face of injustice in order to avoid controversy, which is present in abundance in the parish. Being a gentle person, nurtured by the disciplines of piety, being available to God's grace, which we believe is available to all, is a reality that can come more easily in the parish because it is implicit in one's discipline. That is where the disciplines of piety enter: prayer, scripture reading, and contemplation. This does not mean one will become that graceful person. It does mean the structure is available to bring that reality about. It could be most beneficial if seminars were held on the role of controversy and conflict. I am of the opinion too often the hierarchy does not know how to respond to such. Fortunately I have been blessed with bishops, administrative assistants to the bishop and many district superintendents who have been supportive.

Discoveries

4. My participation in the monastic tradition called me back to my center where, in the midst of the silence, the Divine Presence is found. One must take time. The demands of the parish require it. The discipline of theology informs it.

5. Another discovery that I came to quite late is the importance of community vis a vis the individual. Too long destructive personalities are permitted to undermine the morale of a parish and chip away at its sense of community. In this regard, the Rule of Benedict can be most informative. In The Rule, Benedict does not permit a destructive personality to go unchallenged and disciplined. Many parishes have destructive personalities in them and their destructive ways often go unchallenged. It would be most appropriate to confront, and if need be, to encourage them to leave a community of faith unless they change their behavior. Even our Lord challenged the religious in his time. More than once he challenged the leadership of the synagogues and temple because of their disregard of the marginalized as they clung to the law or tradition. I never thought of telling someone to leave a parish. I would respond to them one-on- one to deal with issues. Nor did the judicatory, including district superintendents discuss this type of relationship and subsequent "excommunication" as our Roman Catholic friends would have it.

6. The beauty of officiating at a funeral in the home is a practice worth visiting. Another is the practice of holding a funeral in the community of faith on a Sunday morning. This would be especially appropriate for long time parish-

ioners indeed for anyone who is a part of the community of faith. I perceive that to do so would be a powerful witness to the world. Think of the impact on visitors if this experience is done with great dignity and professionalism and structured in such a way as to invite the visitors to be comfortable in this community witness to our faith.

7. To enhance the relationship between the local church and the respective conferences, it would be a blessing to hold the ordination of the elders in the local churches. My experience with Bishop James S. Thomas in Webb-Gillett Grove confirms the significance of that action. I would encourage the judicatory to make this a priority.

8. In the face of an injustice, an unkind word, the mocking of another, and in the presence of any form of negation of the other, the pastor must speak. It is an axiom of the human experience that silence is the voice of complicity.

> To remain silent in the face of injustice,
> To remain silent when a truth needs to be spoken,
> To remain silent when words that provoke must be spoken,
> To remain silent is to lose one's integrity.
> That is all we have: our integrity.

9. The world has a way of setting the agenda. It writes our story of civil rights, war and peace, sexual integrity of individuals: (LGBT) Lesbian, Gay, Bi, and Transgender sisters and brothers, the equal rights amendment. The marginalized continue to stand in the wings of our consciousness waiting for attention. This does not mean we run to the latest fad in methodology with screens, casual attire, "cool music," etc. The richness of tradition including the Eucharist and signified worship will be present

Discoveries

beckoning us to recover the riches after the latest cultural "fad" has past. The hungering for meaningful content and dignified structure awaits the return of the seekers.

10. I am persuaded that the lectionary is a most helpful guide if not *the* most helpful source for biblical preaching. For close to 40 years it has been a critical source for my homilies. In addition to that, it provides the congregation with a walk through the Bible, which helps them understand our heritage rooted in the Hebrew tradition.

11. Through my studies and simply seeking to live a life rooted in theology, it became clear to me that all theology begins with experience. Subsequently it evolves perhaps into systematic theological understanding of life and death and, if it becomes a part of the denominations or academic pursuit with authorities assisting in one's interpretation, it could move to the level of dogmatic theology. In this regard the parish pastor must be open to new theological understandings.

12. Being a part of this privileged profession, we have the opportunity to expose our people to beauty, wonder, awe, and mystery. These speak to dimensions of life far beyond the scientific understanding of life.

13. I invite all aspirants to the ministry in the local parish to be prepared for the unexpected, the surprising, and the unplanned. That is to say "be open to the leading of the Holy Spirit." You will never know when she will "visit you" uninvited.

That's What They Are in For!

14. In telling one's stories and addressing important issues in the preaching gives people permission to tell their stories and in many cases bring healing. The painful issue of suicide is one that is kept in the shadows too often. When brought out into the light of day people find healing in relating their struggles over the death of loved ones by suicide. Wounds are then brought to the touch of healing grace. Those who have despaired of life because of the loss of hope in the area of the physical or for whom the darkness has overcome the mind will visit the pastor. Fortunately some states such as Oregon have the "Death with Dignity" act providing a loving structure for persons to control their own death. I believe that is good.

15. I encourage clergy to avoid labeling themselves or permitting others to label them as "prophets." Their position might be better served if they viewed themselves as "critics of the social order." It is a more modest designation not requiring the passage of decades to foster accuracy.

19

Authors and Their Influence

My ministry in the local parish could not have been as fulfilling as it was without the companionship of authors and commentaries whose writings not only nurtured my mind by giving me clarity about the meaning of the scripture but helped me in looking at the world through the eyes of theology and focusing on living out the kingdom ethic in the world. As I think about some of them specific insights have taken up permanent residence in my memory.

H. R. Niebuhr—In *Revelation* he speaks of our concern with too much Jesusology and not enough theology.

Reinhold Niebuhr,—His *Nature and Destiny of Man* speaks of "Christian Realism" which proved to be a challenge to the pacifist mind.

Paul Tillich—In *The Shaking of the Foundations* he proclaims God's acceptance of us unconditionally.

HelmutThielecke—Thielecke challenges any despot who seeks our absolute allegiance.

That's What They Are in For!

Dietrich Bonheoffer—No one can forget his *Cost of Discipleship* and his clarion call of when Christ calls a person he bids him come and die.

William String fellow—His witness as a lawyer at the East Harlem Protestant Parish back in the '60s. His books enriched my interest in social justice. *A Public and Private Faith*, *Free in Obedience*, to name two.

Robert Raines—His witness to equality during the civil rights struggle and the leadership he provided at Kirkridge Retreat Centre in Bangor, Pa.

Robert McAfee Brown—His *Theology in a New Key* is but one book that comes to mind readily. It is seeing theology through the "musical score" of liberation theology.

Gustavo Gutierrez, Leonardo Boff, Rubem Alves, Juan Luis Segundo; Liberation theologians issued a clarion call to tell the poor that God has a bias towards the poor and poverty is not a part of God's plan. Pope Francis can be added to this list de facto if not with his encyclicals as of this writing.

Feminist Theologians such as Virginia Mollenkott who reminded us that homophobia is at core sexism.

Susan A. Ross brought a feminine perspective to the Eucharist.

Henri Nouwen whose writings covered a multitude of subjects on spirituality and L'arche community focusing on being with the developmentally disabled.

Authors and Their Influence

Then there are the activists like Daniel Berrigan, Philip Berrigan, Sister Corita and untold numbers whose names are not written across the pages of history.

These are among those who inspired us in our protestations during the Vietnam War.

Daniel and Philip Berrigan were arrested for pouring blood on the draft files in Catonsville, Maryland. If my memory serves me correctly, they served time in prison at Danbury, Ct. Subsequent to his release and further acts of civil disobedience Daniel became a fugitive on the run for years. He was finally arrested at the home of William Stringfellow on Block Island, New York. In his later years he was ministering to children with cancer in a New York City hospital.

Sister Corita used her artistic gifts with water colors to compliment writings on social justice.

Afterword

Could I have lived ministry differently? More effectively? I doubt it. To raise such questions and seek to answer them is a waste of psychic energy. One's actions and words spoken are linked inexorably to the moment, the circumstances in which the decisions and actions took place.

My life was rich in experiences filled with hundreds of people in communities of faith and beyond. All this happened because of this historical person who walked the dusty streets of a non-descript village in a country crisscrossed by armies.

This one historical personage provided me with venues for a rich life as defined by all that has been recorded in this narrative. To reflect on that connection through the centuries leaves me with a sense of amazement.

Jesus, identified as the Christ connected by the thread of communities Riceville-McIntire, Webb-Gillett Grove, Riverside (Fort Dodge), Valley UMC in West Des Moines, St. Timothy (Cedar Falls) brought me to this moment when memory escorted me down the corridor of time's passing. Thus, this *Pastoral Memoir of a Privileged Profession.*

Appendix A

The Episcopal Leadership

These are the names of the Episcopal leaders of the Iowa Conference during my tenure as a local pastor: Bishops Gerald Ensley, James S. Thomas, Wayne Clymer, and Reuben Job. While serving in the Oregon-Idaho Conference, the leadership included Bishop Ed Paup and Bishop Robert Hoshibata. Although each brought different gifts to the office, the one who stands out as having the greatest influence on my life was Bishop James S. Thomas, whose presence in my life I noted earlier. For the privilege of being a local pastor in a variety of parishes in Iowa and Oregon, I give profound thanks. Have I lived a good life? I hope so.

Appendix B

Reflections

There Is a Way to Be Good Again

"What do you do in the Monastery? We fall down and we get up . . ."

"The Eucharist"—March 2005

"December 25, 2004—Christmas Day"

"An Amazing Place—Faith United Methodist Church"

"Advent is upon us! He is coming soon!"

"Up a Tree"

"Once upon a time"—Ireland / The Wise Woman

"Dublin—Running with the Hares"

"Lent—The Season of Amazing Grace"

"There is a way to be good again!"—The Kite Runner—page 2

"A message from the fallen towers of 9/11/01"
—Ann Nelson

"The Crucifixion of Humanity"

Appendix B

"Letters from Africa"

"Percie's Poems"

"A Personal Note" October 2006

"Yogi Berra, All Saints Day and Money"

"Homecoming" November 2005

"December 2005" Charlie Brown "The Good News Baby"

"Prayer in the Time of Terrorism"—August 2005

"The United Methodists are coming"—Damascus

"Toward a New Declaration of in(ter)dependence"

"The Church of England in Leicestershire"—Stathern, England—August 2008

"The Ministry of Presence—The Monastic Tradition

"Celtic Blessing"—Rostrevor, Northern Ireland

"A Pastoral Letter to the Faith Community" April 2004—Homosexuality

"Remembering"

"The Work of Christmas" January 2007

… Appendix B

Letters from Africa

> Letters from Africa from the Fourth
> and the Twenty-First Centuries
>
> Give testimony to the power of faith to
> sustain us in the midst of fearful times

The time: The middle of the third century (200–300 Common Era).

The place: Carthage, North Africa.

The event: A letter. A middle-age man, Cyprian by name, is writing to his friend Donatus. This is what he says:

> This seems a cheerful world Donatus when I view it from this fair garden under the shadow of these vines. But if I climbed some great mountain and looked out over the wide lands you know very well what I would see. Brigands on the high roads, pirates on the seas, in the amphitheaters men murdered to please the applauding crowds, under all roofs misery and selfishness. It is really a bad world, Donatus, an incredibly bad world. Yet in the midst of it I have met a quiet and holy people. They have discovered a joy which is a thousand times better than any pleasure of this sinful life. They are despised and persecuted but they care not. They have overcome the world. These people Donatus, are the Christians and I am one of them.

The time: January 31, 2004

The place: Kampala, Uganda, Central Africa

Appendix B

The event: A letter from Fr. Gary Smith, S.J., to friends in Portland, Oregon.

> Christmas (2003) began early for me. It started in Adjumani refugee villages ten days before. Christmas: hearing confessions. It is a sacrament that thrives with Sudanese Catholics. I listen to a variety of languages, pray in English and give absolution in Arabic . . . My first day out I was in a village called Muburu and the catechist there, a woman, told me that her aging mother, Yoya, wanted to make a confession; so I was led to mom's little hut and waited. Yoya appeared, blind and crippled. She moved to an empty grain sack on the dirt floor, greeted me and made confession fervently. She is so happy that I was there that you have'd thought Jesus had made an appearance. She grabbed my hands after absolution and gazed into wherever-she-thought-my face was, and gave me a high-octane toothless smile. There was a profound work of art in those sightless eyes. Was I looking into the feminine face of God? Then she sunk into a prayer of thanksgiving (her daughter told what she was doing). It was a heart cracker. I asked the question: Where are the mystics of this world? Are they sitting on crummy sacks on crummy dirt floors in northern Uganda? Among the blind and the crippled?

After writing at length about the beautiful Christmas Eve Mass in a village called Alere and a festive Christmas Day celebration, Fr. Gary concludes his letter with a sense of God's presence not unlike Cyprian of the fourth century.

> My heart is good. There are times, in the extremes of the bush and in the difficult work that

Appendix B

> I stagger. Fatigue, some loneliness. That being said, I trust in God knowing that there are gaps in me that will never be filled. But the most existential gap, the longing to know and serve God is and has been met in a thousand ways. Much peace and love to you both.

The letters of Cyprian in the third century and of Fr. Garry Smith in the twenty-first Century reveal the power of our faith to sustain one in a most fearful world. They both reveal a trust in God. Jesus revealed such a trust in his pre-resurrection world. We are privileged to live in a post resurrection world. We know what happened on Good Friday. And we know what happened on Easter. I invite you as I invite myself to reflect on these two post-resurrection men and their witness to life being stronger than death, and love being stronger than hate, and vulnerability being able to triumph over the defensiveness that leads to suspicion, fear, and possible hatred and violence against those who are "different." What the world needs now is not more killing, not a continuation of our national obsession with war and the ever, ongoing preparation for war. What the world needs now is not the ongoing militarization of the globe to the detriment of the health and welfare of our nation and the world. What it needs now is for us, for you and me to seek to understand and make our own the genius of the good news of God's love for us and for everyone a most inclusive love.

Perhaps one day you and I may be able to write from our "garden" to one who lives in a world where so many are edging towards despair and hopelessness.

Respectfully,

Bob Leverenz

Appendix B

End note: Last week we received a letter from Fr. Gary the closing sentence of which provides an "exclamation point" to his faith, and hopefully, one can make our own in our community of faith.

"Spirit wise I am okay. Just tired. The people continue to give me strength and are God's greatest gift to me and to the Jesuits who blessed my being here."

The Kite Runner

There is a way to be good again caught my imagination on page 2 of this 370 page novel. Buried in the story, this statement has refused to let go of me in this season of Easter. The struggle of the human spirit to be healed of wounds inflicted by others or self-inflicted echoed the truths of our faith.

I am of the opinion that anyone who reads this *Reflection* has had and most likely continues to have experiences which have "cried out" for an opportunity "to be good again," to heal or be healed of a past hurt received or inflicted on another.

This statement compelled me to read the novel because it sets the stage for one's search for an action that might lead to the redressing of an historic hurt. *The Kite Runner* leads us through a horrendous, complex maze of emotional, spiritual, and social complexities in the struggle to be whole. Although it is fiction it is set in present day Afghanistan and the United States.

This statement is the promise that comes with any attempt at healing. It is not unlike statements Jesus had made on several occasions, "Come to me all who labor and are heavy laden, and I will give you rest."

Appendix B

A truth such as this, "There is a way to be good again" could well have haunted the prodigal son or daughter in the far country.

Consider how much hope is connected with the possibility of a new beginning, a new life, a healing within or a "way to be good again"? Think how Peter and the others might have felt when they encountered Jesus' presence in the upper room, behind locked doors and they experienced him saying, "Peace be with you." It staggers the mind to think how Judas might have responded had he heard there is a way to be good again. Imagine how the women felt, those who had gone to the tomb and were first to tell the world, via the disciples, "There is a way to be good again." Jesus is on the loose and "will go ahead of you to Galilee." There he will tell you how being good again is done. In one sense *The Kite Runner* is your story and mine. It "walks" back and forth over the range of human behavior, all of which I'm convinced, you and I are capable.

It is disconcerting to think that might be true. But believing it to be true, it is important that we be grounded in our faith story. Should the tragic conditions of *The Kite Runner* come to our lives, knowing that the fabric of civil behavior is gossamer thin, you and I would be able to stand against the tide of hatred that might well up within ourselves or from the society around us.

Being so immersed in our faith story we would thus be able to:

> Go out into the world in peace.
> Be of good courage,
> Hold fast to that which is good,
> Return no person evil for evil,

Appendix B

> Strengthen the faint hearted.
> Support the weak,
> Help the suffering
> And most surely honor all people.

Remember please, There is always a way to be good again.

During my tenure at St. Timothy Church in Cedar Falls, Iowa I was given the opportunity to provide commentary on public radio at the University of Northern Iowa. I list these for my benefit as well as to reveal the range of topics covered in the mid-eighties. I am including a couple of commentaries to give the reader an idea of their content. It is amazing how the subject matter of the eighties is present with us in the second decade of the twenty-first century.

I consider it a privilege to be able to present these observations as an ad hoc representative of the church.

Appendix C

Commentaries—Public Radio KUNI—1982/87

Humanism

The Arrogance of Power

The Rise and Fall of the Religious Right

A Bus Ride (around Waterloo, Iowa)

Creation and Evolution

The Peace Movement

Can the Traditional Family Be Saved?

Prayer in the Public Schools

Cynicism

Politics & Politicians

The Death Penalty

Homosexual Is My Neighbor

Why Can't a Woman Be Like a Man? (Junior Chamber of Commerce 1982)

Injun Country—Waterloo Park

James Watt & Hope Martin Park

Appendix C

God's Bullies (2/22/83)

Violence and Guns (The Gun—A Household Pet)

Can the Children of Isaac and Ishmael Live in Peace?

To Burn or Not to Burn—3/9/83

The Rhetoric of Reagan—3/20/83

The Holocaust and Silence—9/14/83

Bible Distribution in the Public School Classroom

Violence, the Survival Game

The Role of Religion in Commencement Exercises—6/2/82

Bumper Stickers & Prejudice—in 1982 /83 Japanese Target—Now Muslims ...

The Bible and its use and misuse

Beyond War—2/8/85

Auschwitz, The Holocaust and Remembering 2/1/85 Need of a Scapegoat

Our Backyard—War in Nicaragua

Deceit—Guatemala/Nicaragua

Political Theology **11/07/87

The Statue of Liberty **7/1/86

The Vietnam War Memorial 9/26/86

Suicide 9/12/86—1/21/85

Civil Disobedience—6/6/86

The Intolerance of Christians—Terry Branstad—4/11/86

Name Calling—5/23/86

Appendix C

Dr. Helen Caldecott—5/9 86

Peace on Earth, Good Will towards Men, Women and Children.

"na, na, na, na, na"—11/26/85

The United Nations—10/30/85 ***

Fear—10/9/85 ***

Media Violence: Is It Hazardous to Your Health

Make My Day—3/27/85 ***

Pete Rose—9/12/85

Jerry Falwell & Bishop Desmond Tutu—8/23/85

Patriotism—7/5/85

Totalitarianism on the Rise—6/13/85

Doomsday Religion and the Arms Race . . . 1984

Two Different Worlds

File on the School Prayer Amendment . . .

The Death Penalty in 1985

The Need for Outrage—12/6/84

War Tax Resistance Movement—3/1/85

Disinformation—4/15/85 Reagan Visits Nazi Cemetery

Dressed to Kill—11/9/84

Ronald Reagan Evangelist in Chief—9/21/84

Geraldine Ferraro—7/20/84

War Games Violence and Masculinity

Our Friend the Gun

Appendix C

Martin Niemoeller—4/17/84

The Iowa Caucus and the Republic of South Africa—2/21/84

Tender Mercies & Terms of Endearment

America, a Very Religious Nation

The Recovery of Imagination—1/4/84

The Cabbage Patch Doll's Craze—12/9/83

That's Incredible—11/23/83

The March on Washington—8/27/83

The Debate over Excellence in Education

The President's Response / The Korean Jet Tragedy—9/15/83

A State of Minds

Baseball Revisited—7/7/83

Whatever Happened to Cemeteries? 6/15/83

Human Sacrifice/War

It appears the issues endure through the decades and the struggle continues between progressive and reactionary defense of the indefensible.

Many of the same concerns are with us at this writing (2012). The names of some of the players have changed, but the similarities stand in stark relief. The commentary printed below, though written in the early 80s, has a contemporary ring to it. Thankfully, the wars of our era are winding down, but the peddlers of fear, political ideology, expediency, xenophobia, partisanship, the need to scapegoat: these powerful forces are alive and well in our

Appendix C

day. Will we learn from the past? I have my doubts, but I can still hope because the global community is more interconnected than ever. Technology has created what Dr. Martin Luther King Jr. declared years ago, a world house.

Maybe, just maybe, reason might prevail and the human sacrifice of war will diminish if not relegated to the dust heap of history.

Human Sacrifice/War

It has been my assumption that human sacrifice was a practice reserved for so-called primitive people and primitive religions. Human sacrifice was supported by a belief system, a principle of which was to appease the gods or god. And these traditions had their functionaries, their priests to carry out this deadly business.

My assumption has been shattered. I have discovered that this practice is alive and well in our time. This primitive practice is found in the political arena of this country. Two examples will suffice to support my contention. The first comes from the Vietnam era. The second comes from our nation's actions in recent months.

Recently I found myself reading once again an insightful book by J. William Fulbright titled, *The Arrogance of Power*. In the section dealing with the Bay of Tonkin Resolution of August 7, 1984 Senator Fulbright confesses he was influenced by partisanship not wishing to have a Republican elected believing it would be a disaster for the country. In the light of subsequent events he had come to regret his role in adopting that Resolution.

Imagine that!!! Political partisanship and political expediency led to the sacrifice of over 50,000 U.S. young

Appendix C

people and innumerable Vietnamese, as well as wreaking havoc and death on an entire nation. Political partisanship is the god to whom human sacrifice is made. That god of partisan politics is alive and virile in the halls of Congress and the White House today (1984). Recall the recent debate on aid to the contras. Remember the votes in the Senate and House (52–47), (222–210) respectively, basically along party lines. Pride, fear of embarrassing the President or being embarrassed by charges of being "soft on communism" or worse; these were the dynamics which made up the litany for human sacrifice in those debates.

∼

What is needed are leaders who will refuse to bow down at the altar of political expediency, who will refuse to pay homage to the god of partisan politics.

The confession of J. William Fulbright is a reminder to us to challenge the high priest in the White House and the associate priests in the Congress as they prepare the country for additional human sacrifice, be they Libyans, Latinos in Central America, or United States citizens.

Whatever Became of Cemeteries?
(June 14, 1983)

What ever became of cemeteries? I mean grave yards with head stones standing upright; stones with writing on them other than the dates of birth and death. Writing which would tell us something about the person whose remains rest beneath the sod.

Appendix C

Places where people are buried are still around but they are undergoing a new look and a name change. Now they are called memorial gardens, or memorial parks, or gardens of memory. These places are vast lawns which look different than traditional cemeteries for the grave markers are level with the ground.

There is a certain sameness in these modern cemeteries. There is no variation in the color, size or shape of these plagues marking the graves.

There are no epithets giving us a glimpse of the person buried, or any type of witness to the faith which might have been theirs.

But I wonder if something has been lost. These modern gardens and parks cannot compare in personality to the glories of cemeteries gone by. There is not a single park or garden which can compare to the charm, the stories, the personality of Woodland Cemetery in Des Moines, or Greenwood in Cedar Falls, or Elmwood in Waterloo. Certainly these parks and gardens cannot compare in personality to the old cemetery near the monastery, New Melleray Abbey, south of Peosta, Iowa ten miles from Dubuque.

These old cemeteries tell stories. The names and inscriptions as well as the shape of some of the stones make up the history of a pioneer people.

To wander through these old cemeteries is to take a walk through history. Some of the old cemeteries were so rich in history they would be places to visit on a Sunday outing. Perhaps this trend of name changing from grave yard to cemetery and now memorial gardens and parks is society's latest attempt to deny death. Today's last rites reflect our culture's attempt to streamline, to make every-

Appendix C

thing precise, organized, clinical, controlled, efficient and emotionally neutral. Even the flowers, artificial plastic or silk, promote the illusion of endurance, driving from our consciousness the fact that we will all decay and inevitably return to the dust of the earth.

Perhaps it is impossible to reverse the trend. So I think I will have to look for a cemetery for my burial which will permit a gravestone which will have some writing on it as well as my birth day and death day. Maybe someone will come by and muse on whether my life and death were interesting.

Bibliography

Chittister, Joan. *The Rule of Benedict: Insight for the Ages*. New York: Crossroad Publishing, 2003.

Delaney, Frank. *The Last Story Teller*. New York: Random House, 2012.

Doss, Joe Morris. *The Songs of the Mothers*. New York: Church Publications, 2005.

Hauerwas, Stanley. *Hannah's Child*. Grand Rapids: Eerdmans, 2010.

Heschel, Abraham. *Moral Courage and Spiritual Audacity*. New York: Farrar, Straus and Giroux, 1996.

Killinger, John. *Bread for the Wilderness: Wine for the Journey*. New York: Angels Books, 2012.

Kristof, Nicholas, and Sheryl WuDunn. *Half the Sky*. New York: Vintage Books, 2010.

Lewis, C. S. *A Grief Observed*. San Francisco: Harper, 2001.

Niebuhr, Gustavo. *Beyond Tolerance*. New York: Viking Press, 2008.

Thomas, James S. *Methodism's Racial Dilemma: The Central Jurisdiction*. Nashville: Abingdon, 1992.

The United Methodist Church. *The Faith We Sing*. Nashville: Abingdon, 2000.

www.ingramcontent.com/pod-product-compliance
Lightning Source LLC
Chambersburg PA
CBHW071438160426
43195CB00013B/1949